ROBERT SCHUMANN
HIS LIFE AND WORK

BY
HERBERT BEDFORD

GREENWOOD PRESS, PUBLISHERS
WESTPORT, CONNECTICUT

Originally published in 1925 and 1933
by Kegan Paul, Trench, Trubner & Company, Ltd., London

First Greenwood Reprinting 1971

Library of Congress Catalogue Card Number 70-106712

SBN 8371-3442-0

Printed in the United States of America

PREFACE

METHODS of writing biography may roughly be divided into three classes : the voluminous and redundant, the moderate and readable, the chatty and undignified. The first class appeals to what Nietzsche tersely called " learned idlers," the second appeals to cultured people with an adequate amount of leisure, and the third to schoolgirls, frivolous-minded persons and those who have no taste for " literature " other than that which is termed *light*. In the early and mid-Victorian Age, biographies running into three large volumes, heavy to lift and even heavier to read, were the fashion. They were eminently characteristic of the drab dullness of that—fortunately—bygone age, their dullness being often accentuated through bowdlerisation. Occasionally this type of biography is even to be met with nowadays, when people are busier dancing than burning the midnight oil " over a ponderous tome." A few years ago the life of a celebrated poet appeared in the biographical arena. This poet was a pronounced dipsomaniac, yet his biographer contrived to write his life from start to finish without even once introducing the word soda-water, let alone *whiskey*. Such biographies should come under the heading of fiction, for not only do they fail to fulfil their purpose, but they mislead the public.

In the following pages Herbert Bedford has been guilty of none of the aforementioned biographical defects. His book belongs to the second and best category—the moderate and readable—using that word in its best sense. Nor has he been guilty of misrepresenting Schumann, and painting him with a larger and more luminous halo than he in reality possessed. And in making this statement I may perhaps permit myself to add that at the moment I am especially acquainted with the *ins and outs* of Schumann's life, owing to certain research work I was compelled to pursue in connection with the writing of a book on *The Influence of Music on History and Morals*. In that book I attempted to show that Schumann's music exercised a marked influence on the child-mind, and helped towards a greater unity and understanding between parents and children. If

this is as true as I firmly believe it to be, then
Herbert Bedford's book should particularly
commend itself to all parents and all lovers of
children, as well as to music-lovers in general.

CYRIL SCOTT.

London,
  May, 1925.

CONTENTS

SCHUMANN

CHAPTER I

INTRODUCTION

A SKETCH OF THE ROMANTIC MOVEMENT
IN THE ARTS

IN contemplating such a work as that of a biography of *Robert Schumann*, one finds oneself confronted on all hands with signs of the movement whose full tide swept across the field of all the arts, in greater or less degree, at the beginning of the Nineteenth Century—the movement towards romance in the arts, a movement that was destined to change the aspect of each one of them, and none more than the art of music.

It may be said to have been born of the desire for a greater freedom of expression than seemed at that time to be possible within the scope of the formality that had come to be regarded in all the arts as the classic ideal.

Among the upheavals caused by the French Revolution was the shattering of all confidence in the permanence of the conditions of life, whether national, social, political or artistic ; and this feeling of insecurity of tenure in every direction could only be emphasized, and more completely realized, throughout the succeeding half century.

The Romantic movement may be said to have been born in Germany ; but it is none the less necessary for the understanding of the conditions of the period, to follow and consider the course of events in France, Napoleon being not only the dominant spirit of the age, but one engaged in working out, in his own life, one of the most amazing romances of all time. Engrossed as he was with the kaleidoscopic happenings of his own destiny, and of the French nation, at the cost of every other nation in Europe, the men, women and children of those nations were not so much pawns in a gigantic game of chess, as mere counters for adjustment of the gains and losses of Kings.

The simplest way of crystallizing one's impressions of the instability of conditions on the continent of Europe at the time under consideration will be to glance over the events of the few years that followed the crowning of Napoleon as Emperor of the French in 1804, remarking the incredible swiftness with which events of the utmost importance crowd the one upon the other.

In 1805, after annexing parts of Switzerland and Northern Italy, he crowned himself King of Italy. Pitt forthwith arranged a coalition against him, consisting of Austria, Russia and Sweden; while Spain took the side of Napoleon.

Napoleon pressed forward his preparations for the conquest of Great Britain, but Nelson's victory at Trafalgar over his and the Spanish fleets, caused him to alter his plans. Bringing his armies against the continental enemies, he defeated the Austrians at Ulm, and both the Austrian and Russian armies at Austerlitz.

After these victories he proceeded to reconstruct the map of Europe, compelling Austria to cede the Tyrol to Bavaria, and her Italian territories to France. As a reward for the neutrality of Prussia, Napoleon presented her with the Duchy of Hanover.

He nominated his brother Joseph King of Naples, and his brother Louis King of Holland. He organized the smaller States of Western Germany into the Confederation of the Rhine, under French protection, and the Electors of Saxony and Bavaria he made kings.

In the following year, Prussia, imagining herself sufficiently strong, challenged Napoleon, and was severely beaten at Jena and Auerstadt. Napoleon entered Berlin, and dictated an order of blockade against the British Isles ; this blockade however, was never really an effective one.

In 1807 the Russians were severely beaten at Friedland, and compelled to recognize Napoleon's reconstruction of the map of Europe.

The following year (1808) saw our entry into the Peninsular War with varying success.

In 1809 the Austrians were again beaten, at Wagram, and compelled to an unwilling alliance with France, Napoleon marrying the Austrian Emperor's daughter.

1812 saw the French invasion of Russia, with

its tragic ending; and also saw the outbreak of war between Great Britain and America.

In 1813 Russia, with Prussia and the rest of the German states, defeated Napoleon in the battle of Leipsig.

The Allies crossed the Western frontier of France early in 1814, and the English advanced from the Pyrenees. Napoleon was thereupon compelled to abdicate; and, at the Congress of Vienna, the Allies in turn took in hand the reconstruction of Europe, pushing back the French frontier, and punishing the King of Saxony—who had been the last of the German princes to abandon Napoleon and throw in his lot with the Allies—by giving a large part of his Kingdom, with about a million inhabitants, to Prussia.

Bad habits, even among rulers, are not easily discarded; so it is not surprising to see the Powers once more banding themselves together in new groups, Russia and Prussia standing together in opposition to Great Britain, France and Austria.

1815 saw the return of Napoleon, his campaign of a hundred days, and his final overthrow at Ligny, and at Waterloo.

Once more the European map was redrawn: the French boundaries were put back to those of 1790. Austria was given the Venetian territories in Northern Italy: and the Emperor declared President of the Confederation of such

4

of the German States as had formerly been included in the Holy Roman Empire :

The Netherlands became a kingdom :

Finland, taken from Sweden, was given to Russia :

Norway, taken from Denmark, was given to Sweden ; and Prussia received compensation in Pomerania, Saxony, and the Rhine provinces, for the surrender of part of her Polish possessions.

The foregoing is, of course, the merest bird's eye view of the national events of a crowded ten years of romantic Emperorship, which cannot have been without effect upon the moral and material life of the entire population of Europe. Harassed by wars, and distracted by rumours of other wars, it seems in retrospect not a little wonderful that from among the inhabitants of those smaller German states, lying near to France, or in the route to the more Eastern objectives of the Emperor who forced his hated protection upon them, should have been forthcoming the æsthetic impulse to enter into new problems of Art.

Yet adventurous minds were not slow to feel the need of claiming for art the application of new and wider horizons such as lay open before them in other and more material directions.

A cursory glance at the state of Art in the latter half of the eighteenth century, reveals the classic ideal as permeating it in its various branches. In painting, the influence of Sir Joshua Reynolds, Thomas Gainsborough, William Hogarth, Jean-Marc Nattier, Richard Wilson, Jean-Honoré Fragonard, George Romney, Francisco Goya, Jacques-Louis David, Pierre Prud'hon, in their several individual directions, still held sway.

In literature the influence of Samuel Johnson, who had handed on the Alexander Pope tradition, was paramount in England: in Germany the poetic and æsthetic criticism of Gotthold Lessing, Friedrick Gottlieb Klopstock, and Christoph Martin Wieland, though throwing off the almost overpowering influence of French classicism, still sufficed for the demarcation of conservative boundaries: while in France the Molière-Racine tradition, emasculated though it was by Voltaire, still continued its austere reign.

Music in this country was imitating George Frederick Händel, while on the continent the chief influences came from the works of Christoph Gluck, Joseph Haydn, Wolfgang Mozart and Maria Luigi Cherubini.

In the carrying on of the great classic ideal, the tendency lay towards the glorification of the technique of form, and thus to the emphasis of its formal side, the outer, to the neglect of its inner significance. This, naturally, can be more particularly seen in the work not only of mere imitators, but in the work of all the lesser men to whom it must have been the side of the music most clearly defined, and, therefore, the more easily to be understood and assimilated.

Such being, generally speaking, the classic calm of the arts at the end of the eighteenth century, there were, discernible below the surface, new influences already at work, and others in the making, not only among poets, but among painters and musicians, who sought for greater freedom in the expression of their art than they found to be attainable without breaking away from classic tradition.

Among the painters John Crome, J. M. W. Turner, and John Constable were joined by Jean-Baptiste Corot, Richard Bonington and Honoré Daumier.

In the neighbouring realm Ludwig von Beethoven, the originator of the movement in music, was in due time followed by Carl Maria von Weber, Franz Schubert, Hector Berlioz, Robert Schumann and Richard Wagner.

It is, however, in literature that we must seek the earliest expression of the spirit that underlay the romantic movement. The term " romantic " used in contradistinction to the word " classic," was first applied to chivalric tales of adventure, having for their heroes fantastic knights-errant, moving in a dim world of mystery and imagination, dear to the story-tellers of the middle ages ; and it was these stories, written in old French and Spanish dialects, half forgotten, that became the inspiration of the new movement.

Not only were they translated into German, but their pervading spirit was assimilated; and the new poems and prose works of the originators of the new school were deep-dyed in it.

As applied to German opera, Dr. Philipp Spitta, of Berlin, in an illuminating article, summarized the romantic spirit thus:

" There were, in romantic opera, four principal elements, the imaginative, the national, the comic and the realistic. The fusing of these four elements by means of the imagination into one whole is what constituted German romanticism."

The originators of this literary movement were August Wilhelm von Schlegel (1767-1845), his brother, Karl Wilhelm (1772-1829), Ludwig Tieck (1773-1853), Friedrich von Hardenberg (1772-1801), whom Thomas Carlyle dignified with the title of " the most ideal of idealists," and Ludwig von Arnim (1781-1831).

Probably the works by which August von Schlegel is best known are his renderings of Shakespeare's plays into German, published in Berlin between the years 1797 and 1810. Ludwig Tieck also took an active part in this work, the influence of which upon German literature and upon German poetry in particular was both far-reaching and long-lasting.

We find in the England of that day something of a similar cry for freedom from classic restrictions, in the poems of Sir Walter Scott,

Lord Byron, Percy Bysshe Shelley ; and in still classical France, in the works of Victor Hugo.

We have here, of course, little more concern with the progress of the Romantic movement in its special regard to literature ; but it is not difficult to realize the rapidity with which the new spirit of freedom overflowed its literary boundaries and permeated the other arts, and in particular the art of Music.

Accepting the foregoing as a bird's eye view of the position of Art at the beginning of the Nineteenth Century, it will be convenient to interpose here a further short résumé of the chief historical events up to 1856, the date of the death of Robert Schumann, so as to throw into their proper perspective the succession of musicians and others who carried on the romantic movement.

The five years following the final overthrow of Napoleon constituted a reactionary period throughout the whole of the continent of a Europe exhausted by war.

Threats of revolution, and outbreaks of revolution were not lacking to retard the return of confidence, and in 1820 serious revolutions broke out in Spain, in Portugal, and in the Kingdom of Naples.

Austria ultimately suppressed the latter in 1822, in which year, however, there occurred a rising in Greece against Turkey.

In 1823 France restored the Bourbon King

to the throne of Spain, but her attempted intervention in Portugal was prevented by Great Britain.

1824 saw Turkey, aided by Egypt, undertaking the conquest of the Morea, and it was not until 1827 that Greek freedom was established by the victory of the fleets of Great Britain, France and Russia at the battle of Navarino.

In 1829 Russia forced Turkey to sign the unfavourable treaty of Adrianople.

The following year saw the expulsion of Charles X from France, and the succession of Louis Philippe, Duke of Orleans, elected by the people.

The Southern Netherlands revolted against the Dutch, and became the Kingdom of Belgium.

The Poles rebelled against Russia, and were not subjugated until a year later: there were small but significant insurrectionary movements in the various German states, and the " Young Germany " movement came into prominence. It had for its object the reform of politics, literature and morals. It consisted of literary men, whose writings were promptly suppressed by order of the Diet. International aid was invoked for the extermination of the movement and, among others, the poet Heinrich Heine found it desirable to leave the country.

In 1833 the national alliances were Russia, Prussia and Austria, versus Great Britain and France, the latter being supplemented by Spain and Portugal. The source of the trouble was the Mediterrannean question, including the passage of the Dardanelles in time of war.

1840 brought a new grouping of the Powers: Great Britain, Russia, Prussia and Austria supporting Turkey against Egypt, the latter having the assistance of France.

In 1846, Switzerland was racked with the civil war of the Sonderbund (while France and England stood by, taking opposite sides) and the Federal Constitution was ultimately established.

The years 1848 and 1849 were years of revolution. King Louis Philippe was expelled from France, and a republic set up, under the presidency of Louis Napoleon. There were rebellions in Hungary, Austria and in North Italy, all of which were suppressed by Austria. The Chartist riots took place in London; an insurrection occurred in Ireland; and there were also revolutionary movements in Prussia.

In 1851 Louis Napoleon declared himself permanent president of the French Republic, and in 1852 proclaimed himself Emperor.

In 1854 came the Crimean war, with Great Britain, France and Turkey against Russia.

And now we turn again to the consideration of the Romantic school of thought amid all this political turmoil.

" Romantic " being the antithesis of " Classic ", Gluck, in the middle of the eighteenth century, was considered a romantic; but the critical opinion later in the century accepted him as a classic, and in turn dubbed Mozart and Haydn romantics. The term had not, at that time, the special significance in music that it received a few years later ; but it is obvious that the romantic of to-day may well be the classic of to-morrow.

Accepting the intention in applying the label "Romantic" to a certain type of music, as being an endeavour to differentiate it from the music of the recognized classic type of the period, it is no easy matter to draw a line of demarcation between the two styles, an obvious reason for this being that the one so often overlaps the other, even in the works of a single composer. In vocal music, the idea of classing as Romantic all music which happens to be the setting of romantic words, whether in the form of opera, cantata or song, cannot be maintained ; for it is not difficult to call to mind instances of romantic words being set to music that is anything but romantic in feeling, but, indeed, of rigid formality derived from the slavish imitation of the classics.

The first composer of the Romantic School with which we are dealing, was Ludwig von Beethoven (1770-1826) : but while it has been seen that romance in music had, generally speaking, its genesis in literature, it is difficult to trace in the romanticism of this great genius any such beginning. It seems with him to have been rather that the necessity of widening the range of the expression of his music led him to make his way along lines not dissimilar to those on which, a little later, was destined to run the development of the music of the composers deriving their romanticism from literature.

Beethoven introduced his own adventurous spirit into instrumental music, increasing by its greater freedom not only the expressiveness of the orchestra as a whole, but also the expressiveness of the individual instruments of which it consisted. His additions to the expressiveness of pianoforte music were scarcely less amazing, and the last group of his sonatas for the instrument reflect the spirit of the romantic movement in possibly its most exalted manifestation.

Carl Maria von Weber (1786-1826) was the next exponent of the idea, and with him there can be no doubt but that the romantic movement in literature guided and coloured his musical outlook. He thus approached the idea of romanticism from an angle totally different from that of Beethoven, with much of whose music, indeed, he had, until the latter part of his life, little sympathy.

Weber's muse was always at its best when lending itself to the expression or illustration of some fantastic idea, such as those upon which his operas were built; and, indeed, at least one of his pianoforte concertos (Op. 79) was provided with a poetic basis as complete as that of the symphonic-poems of Franz Liszt. Weber was essentially a dramatic composer, and was practically the first German composer of dramatic music. During his life it exerted a stronger sway over the German people than that of any other composer of his day; and the romantic idea that lay behind it, and of which it was so satisfying an expression, made correspondingly rapid progress in the popular mind. Weber was the friend of many of the poets of his day, including Karl Wilhelm Schlegel, Ludwig Tieck and Ludwig von Arnim, all prominent in the romantic movement: but none the less, his friend Tieck was utterly unable to appreciate his dramatic musical qualities.

Louis Spohr (1784-1859) is sometimes included in the Romantic School; but, despite his kindness to Richard Wagner in his early days, he was so entirely wrapped up in his own music that outside influences in any direction had, for him, little meaning, and I should prefer to describe him as a sentimental classic.

Heinrich Marschner (1796-1861) was a composer who followed the romantic banner of Weber, and one whose reputation stood high in the Germany of his day. He may be considered a disciple of Weber, for whom he cherished a cordial friendship. He survived Weber by some thirty years, but can scarcely be said to have carried the idea of romanticism any further than the point at which Weber left it.

Franz Schubert (1797-1828) though imbued

with the romantic spirit from his earliest pre-
dilections, carried the idea no further in the
larger forms of orchestral music, than Beethoven,
and no further in its picturesque side than Weber.
He bore it triumphantly, however, into the
realm of song, opening new vistas, widening its
horizons, and developing its possibilities of the
dramatic, and of the vivid, in ways entirely new
and his own.

Hector Berlioz (1803-1869) comes next in the
chain, and to him belongs the honour of introducing the new order into French music. The
ultra-classicism that succeeded the French
revolution had gained so complete a hold upon
every branch of French art that the romantic
idea was slow to gain a footing there. No
sooner, however, did it gain a hearing, than it
was taken up with the utmost enthusiasm.

It is worth noticing that through all his
dramatic and bizarre effects, Berlioz still maintained that profound sense of logic that is so
essentially an attribute of the French mentality.
His attitude towards the art of music may best
be described in his own words :

" Musique, art d'émouvoir par des combi-
naisons de sons les hommes intelligents . . .
La musique, en s'associant à des idées qu'elle
a mille moyens de faire naître, augmente
l'intensité de son action de toute la puissance
de ce qu'on appelle la poésie . . . réunissant
à la fois toutes ses forces sur l'oreille qu'elle

charme, et qu'elle offense habilement, sur le système nerveux qu'elle surexcite, sur la circulation du sang qu'elle accélère, sur le cerveau qu'elle embrase, sur le coeur qu'elle gonfle et fait battre à coups redoublés, sur la pensée qu'elle agrandit démesurément et lance dans les régions de l'infini ; elle agit dans la sphère qui lui est propre, c'est-à-dire sur des êtres chez lesquels le sens musical existe réellement."

Berlioz was possessed of a phenomenal sense of orchestral sound, and of the colour obtained by the combination of sounds, and he was thus able to develop the technique of romantic instrumentation that adds so enormously to the interest of his works.

On the works of *Robert Schumann* (1810-1856) I shall have occasion to dwell later, and it will suffice here to recognize in him one of the chiefs of the romantic school.

He developed the application of the new idea to music in almost every branch ; but it is probably in his pianoforte music, and in his songs, that we find it most vividly embodied. He was in close touch with the literary side of the romantic movement and, indeed, his own literary style reflects it.

His outlook upon music, however, was a singularly personal one, and except in very occasional instances, all his music bears this unmistakable stamp of his romantic disposition.

Robert Franz, born five years after Schumann,

adopted the Schumann methods of song-writing ; but, although making valuable contributions to it, cannot be said to have advanced the art. His songs may be said to occupy a position in regard to those of Schumann, corresponding to that of the operas of Marschner to those of Weber.

We now come to the great name of Richard Wagner (1813-1884), who carried the banner of romantic opera to its highest point. Weber was dead before Wagner began to write, but he was the hero of Wagner's boyhood, and his influence can be strongly felt in the earlier of Wagner's works. Although from the time of Gluck (1714-1787) the idea of the relation between drama and music in opera had undergone many modifications, it was Richard Wagner who first enunciated the theory (in " Opera and Drama ") that seeing that music is only one part of the whole means of presenting a dramatic truth in the form of opera, it is illogical to distort the part into the appearance of a greater value than the whole.

The romanticism of Richard Wagner as exhibited in his later music-dramas was something very different from the romanticism of the poets with whom the movement originated ; but I do not propose to carry this survey of the Romantic School of music any further than 1856, the date of the death of Robert Schumann. The most important influence within that period, beyond those that have already been touched upon, were François Frederic Chopin (1809-1849), Joachim

17

Raff (1822-1882, the Swiss composer) and Franz
Liszt (1823-1886), each of whom brought something new into music that tended to widen the
frontiers of Romanticism as they found them.
One cannot but recognize that romanticism of
the type of a Werner or a Childe Harold, unless
supported by a powerful vitality, such as that of
the great masters of either literature or music,
could not fail to degenerate into mere sentimentality; indeed, it would be idle to hold
that this is not what happemed in the case of so
many of the lesser men : for just as the disciples
of Haydn and Mozart seized upon the outward
and formal manipulation of their art and made of
it their ideal, the small men of the time of the
literary invasion of music, seized upon the
romantic spirit, and, uncontrolled by the complete personal technique of the great masters,
allowed themselves to wallow in the sentimentality they extracted from it.

It would be absurd to hold that a line
such as Weber—Schubert—Schumann—Berlioz—
Wagner—shows any such tendency; but its
trend in the case of the lesser lights, the disciples,
is too obvious for it to be necessary to enlarge
upon it here.

We have seen the rapidity with which the idea
of romanticism spread in Germany; but during
the period of growth there were, outside the
circle of musical enthusiasts, widely divergent
influences and interests, some hostile to it, and

some merely apathetic : such men as Gasparo
Spontini (1774-1851), the successful composer of
both French and German opera ; Johann
Hummel (1778-1837), who in his day was supposed
to rank with Beethoven ; Maria Luigi Cherubini
(1760-1844), who carried on the Gluck tradition
in Paris ; Ferdinand Hiller (1811-1885), content
to follow along classical paths ; JosephWolfl (1772-
1812), who at one time challenged the supremacy
of Beethoven as a pianist, and Felix Mendelssohn-
Bartholdy (1809-1847), that extraordinarily gifted
musician, who wielded in his day a power sufficiently autocratic to blind the great majority
of his contemporaries to anything in the way of
his shortcomings.

Outside Germany the most vital musical movement of the early part of the nineteenth century
was to be found in Italy. Italian musicians had
long roamed over Europe, directing operas,
composing them, and in many cases settling in
foreign countries under court patronage. Besides
those already referred to, one may mention :

Nicola Piccinni (1728-1800) :
Domenica Cimarosa (1749-1801) :
Giuseppe Sarti (1729-1802) :
Giovanni Paisiello (1741-1815) :
Antonia Salieri (1750-1825).

This new operatic movement was far-reaching
in its popular effect, and—partly owing, no doubt,
to the prestige of Italian art, already recognized

and valued throughout Europe—the success of the new school was almost instantaneous.

Its originators were Gioachino Rossini (1792-1868), Gaetano Donizetti (1797-1848) and Vincenzo Bellini (1802-1835) ; and to their school must be added the name of the German composer, Jacob Meyer (1791-1863) who, Italianizing his name into Giacomo Meyerbeer, adopted the methods of Rossini with great popular success, and ultimately added to them something of his own.

This School reached its climax with Giuseppi Verdi, born in the same year as Richard Wagner, and in his later life by no means unsympathetic to the Wagnerian theories.

Rossini, on the other hand, with his more restricted outlook, would have nothing of them. On first hearing a performance of " Tannhäuser " he remarked, " It is too complex to be judged at a first hearing : *and I certainly shall not give it a second."*

This breathing of new life into Italian opera had its beginnings in no such poetic unrest as that which saw the birth of the Romantic movement in Germany—in the German Universities : it may, on the contrary, almost be said to have been born in the theatre : but it was none the less genuine than its German forerunner, being, indeed, the natural expression of the passionate Latin temperament, with its joy in song, not in song as an art, but song as a part of nature.

But it was a genuine striving towards expression in no less degree than was the romantic movement in Germany, which was the natural and logical outcome of the brooding spirit that was characteristic of the authors of that movement.

We have seen that Romanticism in music is of many different kinds, probably as many as the people who adopted the idea ; so varied, indeed, is the musical romanticism that can span the gulf that lies between the caressing zephyr of a Schumann and what George Meredith has called the rattling heavens and swaying forests of a Beethoven, that there seems to be scarcely more than a single factor common to them all— that of their insistence that the value of the inwardness of music, its meaning, its soul, is greater, and more vital, than the form adopted by technique for its expression. Romanticism is frequently regarded as a protest against dulness in music : Leigh Henry has written of it as " an attempt to vision and express life imaginatively and decoratively", and there have been other definitions of it, some good and some bad. I shall give myself the pleasure of quoting that of one of the authors of the literary movement, Friedrick von Hardenberg, whose gentle claim was that Romanticism was " the art of surprising in a pleasing way ".

In studying the life of any artist it is always

interesting to see clearly just how far the working part of his life is overlapped by those of other artists who may, or may not, have been influences in it, or who may, in turn, have been influenced by it. Art progresses in cycles, and though one branch of it may react more readily than the others to the necessity of expansion in any direction, the resulting movement, if sufficiently vital, must of necessity react, sooner or later, upon the other branches. To provide an easy means of making such a comparison of periods, I have made, as an addendum to this introduction, a chronological table, embracing a selection of artists in literature, music and painting, pertaining to the period under consideration, and to the previous century that prepared the way. It makes no pretension to completeness, for were that aimed at such a chart would become not only unwieldy, but would, by the very bulk of its comprehensiveness, defeat its own object by being too detailed for easy reference.

In the foregoing introduction, then, I have, without probing Romanticism on its æsthetic side, aimed at outlining something of the genesis of the movement, and have endeavoured to show in its true relation to the whole movement, the special upheaval that it brought into the art of music. Such an outline, taken together with the march of political and national events that formed the setting to the movement, will, I

hope, serve to give some suggestion of the conditions of life, artistic and social, into which,
early in the nineteenth century was born Robert
Schumann, to the understanding and just appreciation of the various facets of whose life I regard
some such survey as the foregoing a necessary
background.

CHAPTER II

BIRTH AND PARENTAGE

THE birthplace of Robert Alexander Schumann was Zwickau, in the circle of Erzgebirg, Saxony.

Zwickau was, in those days, a picturesque little town of some four thousand inhabitants. It had formerly been walled and fortified, but over-flowing those narrow limits, it had spread on to both banks of the river Mulde. It possessed an antiquated citadel of some dignity, a library, a Latin school and three churches, one of them being a fine Gothic edifice dating from the middle of the fifteenth century, famed for its possession of several interesting works of art, notably a fine altar-piece by the old German master Wohlgemuth.

It was an industrial centre, with cloth factories, dye works, breweries, tanneries and chemical works ; but in the early part of the nineteenth century its chief wealth lay in the coal and iron of the surrounding district. It does not, then, seem to have been an ideal city for the birthplace of a musician, and, indeed, the inclinations of most of the members of his family lay in no such direction.

His father, Friedrich August Gottlob Schumann, was a man of strong character who made his own way in a disturbed world, amid unpromising immediate surroundings. Being from early youth devoted to literature, he was never able to follow it as his sole profession ; but he contrived to continue its practice, in varying degree, with his more material preoccupations. He was born in 1773, the son of a protestant clergyman of Gera—in the principality of Reuss, Saxony—whose poverty prevented his giving to his son anything more than the most rudimentary education. At the age of fourteen he bound the boy apprentice to a merchant of Ronneburg ; but from that time Friedrich August never ceased his endeavours to make literature his profession. When a youth of eighteen, he wrote a drama ; and his enthusiasm enabled him, within a year, to master the French and English languages for the purpose of making himself acquainted with their literature.

He was at that time employed as clerk in a cotton factory at Hohenstein ; but the following year saw his removal to the University city of Leipsig, where he went to take up a position in a grocery business (save the mark !). Outside such uncongenial occupation he had already made various attempts to earn money by his pen, though with little success ; but the proximity of the University, with its obvious attractions for the aspiring litterateur, overcame his more prudent scruples, and within a few months, throwing groceries to the dogs, he became a student of the University.

His slender savings could not long bear the strain of this expense, even upon the modest basis that obtained among German students of that economical epoch; and notwithstanding his good fortune in selling a story to a publisher, he was forced to abandon the hopes of a University career, and returned crestfallen to the parental home at Gera. There he wrote some further stories, and sent them to a popular novelist of the day, one Heinse, for his opinion. Whatever he may have thought of the work, Heinse formed an opinion of the writer sufficiently favourable to induce him to offer the lad a clerkship in a bookshop in the neighbouring town of Zeitz. Thither proceeded Friedrich August to take up the work, and there he fell in love. The consent of the lady's father, the Rathschirurgus of Zeitz (i.e., the medical officer to the municipality) was only to be obtained on the disagreeable condition that the attractions of the bookshop be abandoned, and the hateful business of grocery once more undertaken.

But to a lover nothing is impossible; so promptly resigning his congenial employment, he returned to Gera with the intention of earning enough money to start his new venture. This he accomplished by the writing of no less than seven novels in less than two years, and by the selling of them, and it is difficult to say which of these two performances is the more remarkable.

At the age of twenty-two, then, Friedrich

August married Johanna Schnabel (two years his senior) and established himself in Ronneberg as grocer. It was, however, quite impossible that books should ever cease to play an important part in his life, and a circulating library was accordingly added to the business.

It seems probable that his natural tendency led him, consciously or unconsciously, to put more thorough work into his library and book trade, for within four years it successfully ousted the groceries, and one can imagine the joy of Friedrich August, the cheery optimist, the fighter in the face of adverse fortune (extricating himself from the tangles of the cotton factory, finally shaking himself free of the petty sands of the grocery business) at finding himself at last established as a publisher of his own works, and the proprietor of a library and a thriving business in books. The extension of the business, particularly by the publication of an important work on the Campaigns of Napoleon, necessitated its removal in 1808 from Ronneberg to the more important town of Zwickau. There the business rapidly developed ; translations of poems by Sir Walter Scott and Lord Byron were undertaken, and the publication of a newspaper for the Kingdom of Saxony was included in it.

There, in Zwickau, were born the Schumann children, Eduard in 1797, Carl in 1801, Julius in 1805, Emilie in 1807, and Robert Alexander in 1810 ; and there in 1826, after some years of ill-health, died Friedrich August.

He left to his family a prosperous business with three sons to carry it on : Eduard was then nearly thirty, and Carl twenty-five ; but it is not difficult to imagine what the death of a father of such a character meant to his wife and family, and in particular to Robert, then at the age of sixteen, to whom his guidance would have been of inestimable value.

One cannot fail to recognize the enthusiast in him, and whatever may have been the literary value of his writings, Friedrich August had made himself recognized as a notable man in the Saxony of his day. It is a pleasure to see, then, in Robert Schumann's father, a fine character, aiming always at the highest, even if it was beyond his reach ; but after all—

> " A man's reach should exceed his grasp,
> Or what's a heaven for ? "

Robert Schumann's mother seems, in middle life, to have become what we should now call a difficult woman, requiring much humouring.

A young friend of the family described her as being kind, but easily fired to blaze up in anger. None the less Robert regarded her as a paragon of all the virtues, though his letters to her show her to have been subject to moods of uncontrolled depression. We find him later writing to beg her not to make such " dreadful discord in his soul " by her joyless outlook on life. True he writes this in 1828, when he can only picture her to himself as seated eternally in her grandfather's chair, preserving a stony silence: but this was only two years after the death of her husband, and her only daughter. Emilie was of a lively disposition, but was for several years subject to an apparently ineradicable skin-disease that prevented her going about among her friends and enjoying life : she was eventually attacked by typhus, and drowned herself whilst in a paroxysm of fever. Such tragic events may well furnish adequate explanation for the mother's state of mind at that time, but she seems at no later period to have been able to summon sufficient strength of character to enable her to do much else than brood over the past.

No doubt the early years of her married life at the grocer's shop at Ronneburg must have been trying to the daughter of the Rathschirurgus, taken straight from the circle of petty officialdom of a small German town, where the holders of office have always been noted for the living up to the full value of their importance as seen by themselves. These years must, moreover, have proved physically fatiguing, seeing that the young mother had to take an active part in the running of the shop in order to allow the enthusiastic Friedrich August some little freedom for literary work.

Whether, in some unexplained way, she cherished in later life a preference for the fancied security of the abandoned grocery business, one does not know, but she certainly had no leaning towards literature, nor any sympathy with the idea of an artistic career for any of her sons. She held herself severely apart from the encouragement of her pet son, Robert, in his nursery musical development : nor at a rather later date would " the portly lady," as we hear she was, permit herself to enter the music room to hear her boy play the works of Haydn and Mozart on the piano, either alone or in arrangement *à quatre mains*, with his little school friend, Friedrich Piltzing, preferring, apparently, to leave her more artistic husband to be their enthusiastic audience of one.

Chronological Table, showing the overlapping of the lives of some Musicians, Poets and Painters, from 1684 to 1856, the date of the death of Robert Schumann.

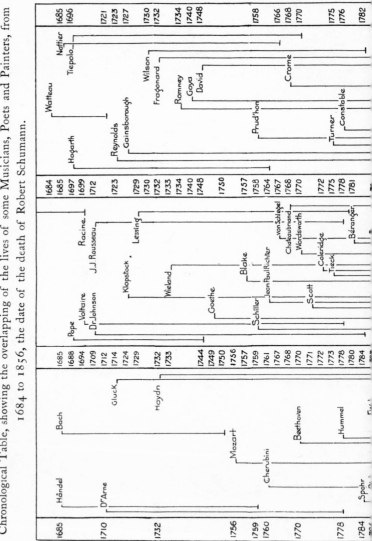

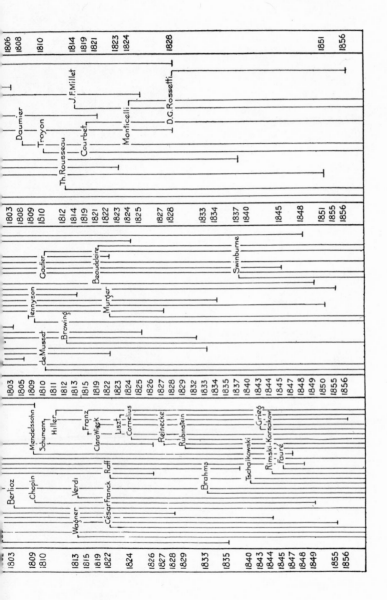

CHAPTER III

1810—1828

ZWICKAU

CHILDHOOD—SCHOOL DAYS

Johann Gottfried Kuntzsch—Ignaz Moscheles—The 150th Psalm—Lyceum entertainments—Literary Club—Death of his father and sister—Agnes Carus—School reading—Jean Paul Richter.

WE have seen that Robert Alexander Schumann was born on 8th June, 1810, in the period when the the Emperor Napoleon was at the pinnacle of his dazzling career, and five years after he had crowned his ardent admirer, the Elector Frederick Augustus, first King of Saxony, of course under the protection of France.

When the child was but two years old, Zwickau lying on one of the routes to Russia, many thousands of French troops poured through the town, followed, at a suitable space, by the Emperor and Empress, with a huge and glittering staff.

Like his namesake the King of Saxony, Friedrich August Schumann was an ardent admirer of Napoleon's genius. He had, indeed, already seen him in person at the town of Gera, and undertaken the publication of Heinse's work upon his Campaigns.

The home atmosphere must have been full of Napoleonic fables, when suddenly the whole fabric came tottering to the ground as the shattered remnants of the French army began to arrive from Russia, famished and frozen, in full retreat before their pursuers, the Russians, soon to be joined by the Prussians.

Severe privations were suffered by the unfortunate inhabitants of Zwickau, most of the food supplies being commandeered for the armies; bread became for a time absolutely unobtainable, and, to make bad worse, an epidemic broke out and spread with alarming rapidity among the population.

Within a few months came the War of Liberation, when Prussia and other German states, aided by Russia, defeated Napoleon in the three days battle of Leipsig (scarcely sixty miles distant from the Schumann home).

After the abdication of Napoleon, and |the dismembering of Saxony by the loss of the northern half of its territory, the Saxon king and the Saxon nation ceased to exert anything beyond a very minor influence among the German states for many succeeding decades.

The punishment inflicted upon the Saxon King, for having dared to be the last of the German rulers to secede from Napoleon, has always seemed excessive; indeed, M. de Talleyrand, the astute statesman who represented France at the Congress of Vienna, is said to have held that the King's only fault was to have allowed his clock to be a quarter of an hour slower than his neighbours'.

At the tender age of four, then, brought up in the house of a man deeply concerned in the stirring events of the day, the nursery life of the small Robert Schumann, without giving him credit for any precocious intelligence, must have been one of intense and varied interest, and the Napoleonic fables of the day a source of the keenest childish enjoyment, resolving itself kaleidoscopically into a series of nightmares as the dreams of victory melted into the reality of defeat.

After a couple of years of nursery tuition in his parents' home, little Robert was, at the age of six (1816) sent to a small private day-school, and there he remained for four years.

Among other things he there learnt something of the rudiments of music. He began to compose at the tender age of seven, and had the advantage of being allowed to borrow music from the Marienkirche, the most important church in Zwickau.

The organist, Johann Gottfried Kuntzsch, gave the boy some instruction, but it is not known precisely when the boy's studies with him either began or ended, nor can it be ascertained that the teacher was either particularly capable or in any way distinguished in his profession. There was, however, none better to be found in the town of Zwickau, and it is certain that little Robert learned from him the rudiments of pianoforte and organ-playing.

Many years later Schumann dedicated to the aged organist his studies for the Pedal-piano, Op. 56, preserving a rather touching affection for his obscure master long after he himself had become famous.

We learn that Herr Kuntzsch's manner was simple but formal; though he seems to have been either unable or unwilling to master his temper when his pupils seemed to him to be particularly stupid. He then resorted to boxing their ears, or even brought a handy blackthorn to bear upon the offenders in the most suitable quarters.

Herr Kuntzsch had a high opinion of his pupil, and did not hesitate to say so when the burning question of a career for Robert was being discussed in his later Heidelberg days.

In 1817, or thereabouts, soon after Carl Maria von Weber received his appointment as Capellmeister in Dresden, Friedrich August approached him with a view to arranging for him to accept Robert as a pupil; but nothing came of it. There seems to have been a general tendency, not only to belittle poor Kuntzsch, but also to minimise his influence over his pupil; but the fact remains that, whatever the instruction may have been that was imparted to the budding genius, in these early but not unimportant years, it came from Herr Kuntzsch, and from nobody else.

Friedrich August lost no opportunity of encouraging his promising son, and took him, at nine years of age, to Karlsbad, no small journey in those days of travel by *diligence*, so that he might hear the great pianist Ignaz Moscheles.

Moscheles was then in his twenty-fifth year, and had recently started on the virtuoso career that carried his name triumphantly through the length and breadth of Europe. The effect of his playing upon the boy was so great that it remained an active factor in his musical outlook for many years.

At the age of ten Robert was withdrawn from his private school, and passed into the Zwickau Lyceum. He spent the next eight years at that school, ultimately passing out in 1828, duly qualified for the University career for which his father had always intended him.

We hear little of his school studies; but with the run of his father's books, and an innate love of poetry, there is no doubt but that his education progressed as much out of school hours as within them. We hear of his essaying poetry, and of his being entrusted by his father (in 1824) with the writing of a few literary sketches of Great Men of the World, a series which he published with much success under the title of *Bildergallerie der berühmtesten Menschen aller Völker und Zeiten.*

Friedrich August took the keenest interest in the education of his sons, frequently discussing literary subjects with them and impressing upon them the importance of the study of foreign languages. For the elder sons there would eventually be his business; but he recognised early in his youngest son, Robert, a spirit of a more original cast, that seemed likely to fit him for an artistic career of some kind. He realized, moreover, in a convinced way that was far from usual in those days, that literary knowledge would not fail to re-act beneficially upon the practise of any art.

To encourage the musical side of his son's education, Friedrich August procured a grand pianoforte, on which, with the co-operation of his young school friend, Friedrich Piltzing, Robert made the acquaintance of many compositions *à quatre mains*, such as those of Czerny, Hummel and Weber, and we hear of him also making other four-handed arrangements, choosing for the purpose the symphonies and overtures of Haydn and others for performance by Piltzing and himself.

Music making in the Schumann home was not, however, limited to pianoforte music, and we hear of the performance of both vocal and instrumental music, when friends of the family furnished such string or other parts as were available, leaving Robert to fill in the remainder at the piano from the score.

We do not hear of Herr Kuntzsch taking part in these performances, and it is likely that about this time he found that his pupil had outstripped him, at any rate in practical musicianship, and gave up the futile task of trying to instruct a pupil who could not only argue with the master but prove himself to be in the right.

In these boyhood days the most ambitious composition of Robert Schumann was a setting of the 150th Psalm for voices and several instruments; beyond the fact of its composition, however, nothing is known of it.

At the age of eleven, Robert took part in a musical festival held in the Church where Herr Kuntzsch was organist. The work given was the *Weltgericht* of Friedrich Schneider, composed in 1819, and conducted by Kuntzsch, with Robert at the pianoforte.

Meanwhile in the Lyceum records of entertainments provided by the pupils, we find the name of Robert Schumann frequently appearing, both as pianist and as a reciter; while in 1825 his name appears as an original member of a Society for the study of German literature, formed from among the students. The statutes of of the Society proclaimed, uncontrovertibly enough, that "for every man of culture the knowledge of the literature of his country is a duty."

In recognition of this principle, the Society adopted a programme for its meetings, consisting of the reading of plays and other masterpieces in verse or prose: the reading of the biographies of authors; and the declaiming of poems composed by members of the society; each item in turn becoming the subject of discussion. In the organization and at the meetings of this Society Robert Schumann took an energetic and prominent part; so indispensable, in fact, were his services, that the Society expired as soon as Schumann's term at the Lyceum came to an end.

During the last years of his life Friedrich August's health, never very robust, passed from bad to worse. Gout had compelled him to pay periodical visits to various watering places, but his passion for work prevented any cure from giving him any lasting benefit. Finally, with his last literary labour unfinished, a translation of Byron's poem, *Beppo*, he died, in August of 1826.

This was a terrible year for Robert, for it also saw the tragic death of his sister, Emilie, which cannot but have been a stunning blow to one of his sensitive nature.

However, the resilience of youth is one of its marvels, and in the following year we find him in full pursuit of the *ignis fatuus* of a sentimental attachment to a young married woman.

Among his father's friends who had occasionally taken part in the concerted music of the Schumann's home, was a wealthy manufacturer, one Carl Carus, a fair performer on the violin, and also on the bassoon. It was at his house, Schumann tells us, that he first became acquainted with the string quartets of Mozart, Haydn and Beethoven, being invited from time to time to undertake the piano part in the Chamber music beloved by his host.

In this year, 1827, a nephew of Carl Carus, one Dr. Ernest August Carus, a medical practitioner of the neighbouring town of Colditz, brought his young and attractive wife on a visit to his uncle's house. She being artistic and generally musical, it was not long before the romantic Robert discovered in her the kindred spirit of whom he had always been in search. Pianoforte duets led to mutual revelations of each other's musical prowess, and the songs of Franz Schubert, and Robert's own compositions helped the development of the romance into which, however, the husband was admitted.

Robert set a number of his own verses to music for her ; but whatever he may have thought of them at the time of their interpretation *à deux*, he apparently destroyed them all at some later date.

In due time Robert was invited to visit the Carus' musical mènage at Colditz, and he spent his holidays there, listening enraptured to the sympathetic performances of his friend, and sure in his turn of an enthusiastic audience for his own. Here he received the pseudonym of Fridolin, a promising pet name borrowed from Schiller's ballad.

This was his first calf-love, and after its first

period of blameless existence, renewed later in Leipzig, where the lady had become a professional singer, it died a tranquil death, devoid of drama, and devoid, too, of anything disagreeable.

1827 was the last year of his school life at Zwickau, but little is known of his school studies in the Classics, except that he read Homer's *Iliad*, practically the whole of Sophocles, Cicero's works (which he loathed) and Plato's, which he liked little better. Sallust, Tacitus, and Cæsar generally attracted him ; but Horace he found particularly difficult, the point of view being utterly foreign to anything in his own nature ; his inclination leading him to the moderns, to the people of a period more nearly in tune with his own. At this time, then, we find him reading Jean Paul Richter's romance, *Der Titan ;* and going from this to his other works, he promptly became an enthusiast for that author, and quoted him to his friends in season and out of season. Until now his favourite poets had been Lord Byron, who had just given his life in the romantic cause of the Greeks against their Turkish oppressors, and Friedrich Schiller, who had then become almost a classic.

Beyond these great names we find that his preference at this period lay in the direction of the works of the lesser men in literature, the minor poets of the day, such as J. S. Seume, Franz von Sonnenberg and the sentimental Schulze.

Such may be accepted as indicating the literary outlook of the boy Robert at the age of seventeen, and it will be found that although with time and experience he extended its horizons, the aspect of his outlook, to which he had largely been guided by his father, remained practically unchanged throughout the remainder of his life.

Here is a free translation of the boy's rather self-conscious reflection on leaving the Lyceum for the last time :

" Behind me lies the school, and before me spreads out the world. Tears well up in my eyes at the thought of coming here no more; but my joy in the thought of the future is greater than the memories of the past. Now must the man within me stand forth and prove his worth for here I stand on the very brink of life, launched into the world of night without a pilot. But as I stand here on the brink, never has the world seemed to me more lovely, as I face its storms with a smile."

Chapter IV

1828—1829

Gottlob Rudel—Leipzig preparations—Gisbert Rosen—Dr. von Kurrer—Heinrich Heine—Bayreuth—Frau Paul—Zwickau —Leipzig —Marschner—Gottlob Wiedebein—Friedrich Wieck —Clara Wieck—Johann Sebastian Bach.

At the death of Friedrich August Schumann in 1826, it was found that he had, by his will, appointed a wealthy friend, one Gottlob Rudel, to act as guardian to his son Robert. During the remaining eighteen months of his term at the Lyceum, the guardian had no particularly important part to play in the life of his ward. After that, however, the position became somewhat different, for owing to there being no instructions in the will as to Robert's career, it naturally became necessary for the Guardian's consent to be obtained before any fresh step could be taken.

No time was lost in deciding upon Robert's entering the University of Leipzig; and the prospect of so doing pleased him greatly. Both mother and guardian were agreed, however, that his ultimate career should be the Law; but this prospect pleased him not in the least.

The mother had always been firmly averse— one need not say obstinately averse—to Robert's wish, often and unmistakably expressed, to become a musician; and now, reinforced by such a man of business as Gottlob Rudel, she had every expectation of being able to impose her will upon her eighteen-year-old son.

Robert accepted the immediate prospect of University life with a good grace; and, accordingly, within a few days of the end of his final term at the Zwickau Lyceum, he was despatched to Leipzig to make for himself the necessary arrangements. There he duly matriculated on 29th March, 1828, entering as *Studiosus Juris*: and secured for himself a couple of handsome rooms on the first floor of a commodious house on the *Brühl*.

They were furnished with unusual elaboration for students' rooms, and were provided with a good grand pianoforte.

Before taking up his residence at Leipzig for the purpose of preparing himself for what his fond mother and deluded guardian had determined should be his life work, it was arranged that Robert should make a short tour in Bavaria to see some of its historic cities.

This expedition was made all the more attractive by reason of his providing himself with a thoroughly congenial travelling companion, in the person of Gisbert Rosen, a young student of Leipzig University, who was on the eve of transferring his studies to Heidelberg, when Robert had the good fortune to meet him. The two young men had many tastes in common; and finding at the outset that they shared mutual admiration for Jean Paul Richter and all his works, they speedily set about the discovery of other points of sympathy, thus beginning a devoted friendship.

Gisbert Rosen readily fell in with a plan which, though doubling the length of his journey to Heidelberg, promised to make it far more than doubly diverting.

Together they duly visited the city of Nuremberg, with its double ring of fortified walls, and rich in the characteristics of the wealthy Burgher class of the medieval Germany.

Travelling south, they reached Augsburg, where Robert presented a letter of introduction to Dr. von Kurrer. The doctor had been one of Friedrich August Schumann's best friends, and Robert repaid the compliment by falling in love with his daughter Clara. His host not only extended his hospitality to the young travellers while they were at Augsburg, but also furnished them with a letter of introduction to Heinrich Heine, to be presented when the travellers reached Munich, where the poet was then living.

In Munich they were well received by Heine, who, though then scarcely thirty years of age, was already famous; but despite the compliment of such a reception to a couple of raw students, Robert Schumann described the poet's manner as being cynical and repulsive. Little

idea had either of the two at that time that
Robert Schumann was destined to exalt the fame
of many of Heine's poems by his musical settings,
and they seem to have parted without regret
on either side.

At Munich the two travellers were compelled,
reluctantly enough, to separate for a time,
Gisbert Rosen having at length to make a straight
line for Heidelberg, leaving Robert to make his
way home alone. During their travels together,
Rosen had contrived to communicate to his
impressionable companion something of his own
enthusiasm for Heidelberg, and his opinion of its
superiority to Leipzig; and Schumann needed
little pressing to determine that no great period
should pass before he rejoined his friend there.

Robert planned his homeward route so as to
include the ancient town of Ratisbon, on the
Danube; a city which, after a series of com-
pulsory changes of allegiance during the period
of the Napoleonic campaigns, had finally become
Bavarian. He then made a pilgrimage to
Bayreuth, formerly the capital of the principality of
Upper Franconia and full of historical associations.
But it was not these that attracted our traveller
there, but rather the fact of Bayreuth having been
the town that his adored Jean Paul had sanctified
by his presence for some twenty years. His death
had occurred there little more than two years
previously, and his widow still dwelt there. In
Bayreuth, then, Robert indulged his sentimental

enthusiasm to the utmost extent ; and not unnaturally seeking an interview with the widow, was rewarded by the present of a portrait of the poet which he carried off in triumph.

From Bayreuth he made his way home possessed by thoughts of Jean Paul Richter, whose philosophy seems none the less to have brought the student home to Zwickau in a difficult frame of mind. For ignoring the natural entreaties of his mother and the other members of the family for some account of his travels to places that none of them had seen, the wilful lad insisted upon repacking his valise forthwith, and within three hours was ensconced in the corner of the *diligence* on his way to Leipzig.

There he arrived, without incident, and proceeded to settle into his rooms. He had provided for his desk three portraits : his father, Napoleon, and Jean Paul Richter ; and of the three it was the poet who was the god of his idolatry, and after whose fashion he set about the task of fashioning his daily life.

No sooner had he arrived in Leipzig, than we find him expressing himself as thoroughly dissatisfied with it. Within a week, in a letter to his mother, he complains that there is nothing of nature to be found in Leipzig, everything is art ; and everything is defaced by art : " Not a valley, not a hill, not a wood where I can abandon myself to my musing—no place where I can be alone, except my bolted room, with everlasting noise and racket below. This it is that makes me dissatisfied."

This everlasting noise must not be mistaken for the student's racket; it was merely the normal bustle of the town : but indeed it seems probable that the root of the trouble lay in himself, and that any place except Heidelberg, no matter whether town or country, would have been equally distasteful to him. He had arrived at Leipzig with what Americans call a " grouch " ; and was determined that in nothing of his surroundings would he find pleasure.

He wrote to his friend Gisbert Rosen, " O, to be with you in Heidelberg ! This Leipzig is a horrible hole—Perhaps, as I write, you are among the ruins of some old castle, happy amid June blossoms ; while I can only contemplate my shattered dreams, and gaze into my cloudy future with tears in my eyes ". His letters of this period are full of expressions of self pity, dangerous enough if genuine, but in this case one feels they are largely affectation. He indicates as much in another letter to young Gisbert Rosen where he writes, " After such exhausting outpourings, you cannot expect me to keep up the strain much longer."

None the less, the general tone of the student life of Leipzig, the Burschenschaft, seemed to the sentimentalist " far too low " to tempt him to take a part in it ; and although he told Rosen that it filled him with horror, he seems to

have had little reason to expect to find anything very different in Heidelberg, where he
had already determined to join his friend after his
first year.

And now, in reading his letters of this time,
we come face to face with the utter inability of
Robert Schumann at the age of eighteen, either
to realize the value of money, or to have even
the primary ideas of managing his supplies. While
this is by no means unusual in the case of young
men experiencing for the first time the sense of
the freedom that is one of the happy con-
comitants of University life, it is generally the
fault of the parents; and in this case if the fault was
attributable to them, they must have been
exceptionally fatuous in their treatment of
Robert in regard to anything appertaining to
money; for while on the one hand he could be
extravagant without the remotest possibility
of squaring his extravagance with his monthly
allowance of twenty-five thalers, he seems to have
been devoid of any feeling of humiliation when
resorting to begging money from any relation or
acquaintance from whom he saw any chance of
obtaining it. He was an expert writer of
begging letters, with a positive talent for the
choice of the method of attack most likely to meet
with success in different quarters. On at least
one such occasion we find him cajoling his guardian
with an assurance that he had finally decided to
accept the Law as his profession.

Far too many examples of his begging letters are still extant for it to be any pleasure to quote from them; but it is an unpleasant fault of Robert Schumann's character at this period that cannot be overlooked, and cannot be explained away.

Like many another youth, he had a great liking for champagne; and whether or not he could pay for it, it was frequently one of his extravagances, unless indeed it was only a silly piece of braggadocio to make it appear so in his letters.

In his first term he made but four friends among the Leipzig students. I quote the following from a letter, translated by Professor Frederich Niecks*: " I go regularly to University lectures, play piano two hours every day, read a few hours or go for a walk—these are all my pleasures. In a neighbouring village, Zweynaundorf, in the loveliest part of all the surroundings of Leipzig, I have often been whole days alone, working and poetizing. So far I have had no close intercourse with a single student. I fence at the fencing school, am friendly to everybody while maintaining my own dignity; but I am most careful about making closer acquaintances; without being repellent one can assume a certain air with such people, so that they keep at a distance, and do not treat one as a freshman."

* Supplementary and corrective Biography of Robert Schumann.

But after all he *was* a freshman and, it would appear, a priggish one at that.

In another letter to Gisbert Rosen, we find* " Excepting Moritz Semmel and Emil Flechsig, Wilhelm Götte is the only man with whom I am at all intimate. I can't say much for the others, and don't pay much heed to any of them unless it be Schütz and Günther, and they are very one-sided." He evidently took himself *very* seriously.

Outside the student circle he was less unsociable; and he became a constant visitor at the house of his friend Agnes Carus and her husband, the doctor, who had now removed to Leipzig. Madame Carus had taken to singing in public, with considerable success, and this naturally brought to their house a constant succession of musical people, to whom Robert (still " Fridolin ") was introduced. Here he had the good fortune to meet Heinrich Marschner, one of the followers of Carl Maria von Weber in the romantic movement in opera; and a composer, who like Robert, had been first destined for the Law.

Another whom he met there was a composer of some repute in his day, Gottlob Wiedebein, Capellmeister at Brunswick, who had made some of Jean Paul Richter's " mystic utterances " the basis of some tone-pictures which Robert thought " glorious beyond all praise."

* F. Gustav Jensen, translated by May Herbert, *Life of Robert Schumann told in his letters.*

To him then, *en amateur*, Robert Schumann dispatched some of his songs, settings of poems by Andr. Justinus Kerner, and was so delighted with Wiedebein's reply, that he at once wrote to say that he should from that moment enter seriously upon the study of composition.

Wiedebein showed an unerring instinct for the recognition of the promise of genius in an unknown amateur; and as it has since become something of a classic, I will give a free translation of the letter he sent to Schumann:

" Honoured Sir,

" Your letter has given me great pleasure, and I shall repay your confidence in my opinion by giving it with complete frankness. There are errors in your compositions, but they are the errors of youth—not errors of the spirit—and can be overlooked in the presence of the pure poetic feeling that pervades your music. That is what pleases me in it.

" In these errors, I discern obvious uncertainty in matters of technique, but I expect, later on, you will understand better what I refer to.

" In the act of composition we abandon ourselves utterly to our inspiration; but later our critical faculty must be brought in to blot out with relentless paw anything of the earth that should have no place there.

" Wild flowers may be allowed to grow up wild; but nobler plants deserve cultivation, just as a good vine must not only be encouraged by cultivation, but also pruned . . .

" Beyond everything, look to truth; alike in melody, in harmony and in expression; that is poetic truth. If you cannot feel it in any composition, then destroy it, even if you love it.

" Examine, then, first the prosody of a song, then your melody and harmony, and lastly the spirit of the whole work which should give it life. If you find that each of these parts fall into its place, giving you the impression of having created out of these factors an artistic unity, then do not bother about what anybody says of it, you will have raised the veil.

" If you have the smallest doubt about it, then, believe me, error must have crept in.

" You are greatly gifted ; use your gifts, and you will prosper in your career."

The kindness and the value of the sympathetic insight, shown in this letter to a young composer, cannot easily be overrated, and that it meant much to Schumann is demonstrated by his having printed the letter some ten years later in his *Neue Zeitschrift für Musik* as an example of what criticism of youth, by age, should be.

To his friend, Frau Carus, he owed also his introduction to Friedrich Wieck, who was an important personage in Leipzig musical circles, and it was at her house too that he first heard his future wife Clara, Wieck's nine-year-old daughter, play as a prodigy.

Friedrich Wieck apparently took a fancy to Robert, for within a few months of his arrival in Leipzig, he became a constant visitor of Wieck's house, and indeed began to study the pianoforte under his guidance. That Friedrich Wieck was an excellent teacher is well known, and proved by known results. He was widely read in the music available for the piano, but was autocratic, argumentative and sarcastic. He seems to have enjoyed being rude ; and, using rudeness as one of his chief weapons, gave offence with no unsparing hand.

As a teacher he must have been trying, "sometimes wild as a boar," said Robert Schumann, but he was nevertheless admired and esteemed by his pupils. He was the inventor of no fantastic pianoforte method, and having nothing of the virtuoso about him, made no claim beyond the possession of special insight into the question of sensitive musical interpretation. He was exceedingly thorough and made a study of the art of singing, which doubtless helped him in his understanding of the subtleties of cantabile playing.

When Robert Schumann first met him, Wieck was a man of forty-three, living in Leipzig with his second wife, his daughter Clara, aged nine, and two other children of his first marriage.

He had made himself respected in the musical

world of Leipzig, for although he forced his opinions forward tactlessly and rudely, they were generally found to be right.

Beyond the music, then, that was made at these two houses, of Frau Carus and Friedrich Wieck, where Robert Schumann had the *entrée*, he engaged in a certain amount of chamber music, *en amateur*, with student friends. The death of Franz Schubert in this year may possibly be accountable for their giving special attention to his string quartets, but Schumann was already a devoted admirer of Schubert's songs. Being at the imitative age, he naturally followed in Schubert's wake by composing not only a set of songs to verses by Lord Byron, but also a quartet for strings and piano, and a set of eight polonaises for piano *à quatre mains*, all of which, however, he suppressed later.

In this year Schumann began the intimate study of the works of Johann Sebastian Bach, and always held them to have been one of the greatest musical influences of his life.

Though it appears from his letters that he occasionally attended the celebrated orchestral concerts at the Gewandhaus, it seems probable that at that period orchestral music occupied a section of his musical horizon, far smaller than that of piano music and chamber music generally.

Meanwhile his legal studies were neglected, although one might not readily have gathered the fact from his correspondence with his mother and

guardian. Having informed the latter that he
had definitely made up his mind to apply himself
to the study of jurisprudence as his profession,
within a few days we find him writing to
Gottlob Wiedebein that he has made up his mind
to apply himself to the study of composition.

He was still absorbed in his enjoyment of
Jean Paul Richter's works, delighting in throwing
off Jean Paulisms in his own letters, and imitating, so far as in him lay, the fantastic mode of
thought and the mannerisms of his ideal poet,
with whose romanticism, with its fanciful hover-
ing over the borderland between tears and
laughter and with its exaggerated self-absorption
he had both by nature and inclination much in
common. Indeed these remained throughout
his life among its chief influences.

He had a few love affairs inseparable from his
condition ; his references to them in his letters
are not particularly edifying ; but, though sometimes in bad state, they are not ill-natured.
They were nothing more than the normal affairs
of sentiment that come naturally enough in the
way of susceptible youth in any age : indeed,
considering his super-sensibility, and the environ-
ment of a University town, it was probably the
good influence of his friend Agnes Carus that
kept him out of more serious trouble.

Throughout the whole of his year in Leipzig,
Robert had been looking forward to joining his
friend Gisbert Rosen in Heidelberg ; and,

having obtained the necessary parental consent, he quitted Leipzig at Easter 1829, and returned home to stay awhile with his family before setting out afresh.

He seems once more to have been in a hurry to start on his journey, but in no hurry to complete it; and after reaching Frankfort was content to travel in leisurely fashion, even though his destination was the city of his dreams.

CHAPTER V

1829—1830

A letter from Zwickau—Wilhelm Häring—Heidelberg—Professor Thibaut—Rosen and Semmel—Töpken—Italian Tour—Heidelberg again—Piano study—Paganini—Piano variations, Opus I—The career of pianist decided on—End of term—Trip down the Rhine—Leipzig again.

A LETTER that Robert Schumann wrote to his friend Gisbert Rosen in Heidelberg, on the last day of April (1829), on the eve of setting out upon his journey, throws sufficient illumination upon his manner of regarding several matters of interest, to warrant my quoting parts of it here in free translation :

" All my castles in the air came perilously near falling in pieces, owing to my brother Julius being taken dangerously ill. For, had he died, my mother would have been left quite alone, and she begged me in that event to remain at home here with her. Luckily the worst is over now, and I can confidently look forward to being with you within three weeks.

" It was a terrible struggle finally to quit Leipzig ; for a girl's beautiful soul had enslaved me. Difficult as it was, all that is now behind me ; my tears are dried, and I am looking forward, full of hope, to the ideal life of Heidelberg.

57

" Did I mention to you that as soon as he has passed his examination at Leipzig, our friend Semmel will join us in Heidelberg ? What a time we three shall have together ! And Michaelmas in Switzerland ! . . .

" We had a great concert here (Zwickau) a couple of days ago with an audience of eight hundred or a thousand people. Of course I played at it, and have been busy making merry ever since ; concerts, suppers, lunches, dances, quartet parties, and to-night a farewell ball, and, luckily for me, all free.

" As soon as I reach Frankfort I shall be able to let you know just when I shall be in Heidelberg. From here I have to go to Leipzig to settle up a lot of debts ; but I shall positively leave there on the 11th, though I shall have very little money left ; perhaps *you* will be able to help me through at first. It is snowing hard here, and I hope I shall not have to finish my journey to you *in a sleigh*. But I am forgetting that with you the spring has probably arrived already, and you are surrounded with colour. To picture it all, positively makes my eyes ache ! I look forward to seeing you again, and the pleasure of our meeting shall compensate us for our long separation. Let the Spring overflow your soul, and dismiss Winter."

He signed himself to Rosen as " your brother," and it is obvious that he was in a more buoyant frame of mind than any in which we have yet seen him.

The first part of his journey, one of over two hundred miles by *diligence*, brought him to the town of Hanau, in Hesse-Cassel, where Napoleon routed the allies in a hard fought battle on his retreat from Leipzig. Thence to Frankfort. The most interesting of the various travellers with whom his long *diligence* journey brought him in close contact was William Häring, whose romance, Walladmor—written under the *nom de guerre* of Walibald Alexis—in imitation of those of Sir Walter Scott, had made him famous all over Germany. This dexterous production, which he announced as being his *translation* of a hitherto unknown novel by Scott, met with extraordinary success, and was for a time generally accepted as genuine, and had been translated into various languages, when Robert Schumann met him. Though twelve years his senior, Häring was evidently attracted to the lad, and the two spent several days together in Frankfort, where the novelist introduced Schumann to Ferdinand Rees, and Frau Rees, who happened to be beautiful enough to set the impressionable Robert buzzing.

The influence of Wilhelm Häring upon his young friend was entirely for good ; and though without doubt the prospect of Heidelberg made him more readily receptive of the influence of the elder's genial and amusing personality, it was

probably something of a revelation to Robert
that anybody capable of distinguishing himself
in literature, could be anything but wrapt in a
theatrical atmosphere of heartbreaking gloom.
Häring awakened something in Schumann's
nature hitherto dormant ; so that learning the
possibility of enjoying beauty without tears, he
became as merry as became his years, and as elated
as became his surroundings. He threw aside his
posing and his self conceit, and his letters became,
at any rate for the time, charmingly unaffected.

It happened that Häring was bound for the
Rhine ; so, nothing loth, Robert changed his
route, and with his new friend, sometimes afloat
and sometimes on land, saw and enjoyed the
beautiful Rhine country from Mainz to Köln,
the two parting company at Coblenz, after an
amusing musical buffoonery at the hotel, with
Robert in his best humour.

We have seen from his letters to Gisbert
Rosen that Schumann had every expectation of
beginning his term at Heidelberg with no super-
fluity of cash ; but he had, when writing, no
idea of entering the city absolutely penniless.
Yet this is what happened ; and, indeed, he was
forced to cover the last dozen miles, from Mannheim to Heidelberg, on foot, entering the town
late in the evening of the 21st May—probably
tired, but certainly happy.

Heidelberg, in the Grand Duchy of Baden,

was formerly the residence of the Electors Palatine, and is chiefly famous as being the oldest university town in Germany.

Built at the extremity of the Grisberg mountains, with the river Neckar flowing below, its position is at once romantic and picturesque.

The place had a somewhat astonishing effect upon the impressionable Schumann—and it looks as though he almost made up his mind, for once, to take the study of Jurisprudence seriously in hand. The principal lecturer was Anton Friedrich Justus Thibaut, a famous teacher whose presence brought many students to the University. To judge from the following extracts from a letter, Robert made at any rate a promising beginning:

" I rise at four o'clock every morning; the sky is ravishingly blue; until eight I busy myself among pandects and private law: from eight to ten we have lectures from Thibaut and Mittermayer: from twelve until it is time for dinner I walk in the streets; from two to four more lectures on law by Zacharia and Johannsen; then to the Castle or to the Rhine or to my beloved mountains."

Now Professor Thibaut himself was not only a legal luminary, but also a musical celebrity, who, four years before Schumann arrived in Heidelberg, had published a short book, *The Purity of Musical Art*, in which he delivered a spirited attack upon the degeneration of Church

Music in Germany. Possibly, then, Professor
Thibaut's known musical sympathies may have
been an influence sufficient to evoke in the
pupil, at any rate at the beginning of his first
term, some little interest in his legal studies.
But if that were so, it was not strong enough to
hold him long interested in the study of a subject
which, despite an occasional spurt to which the
spur of impecuniosity pricked him, was thoroughly
antipathetic to his whole nature. His attendance
at lectures soon became spasmodic and irregular,
and a greater part of his time was given to music,
and to the study of French and Italian. His
principal friends were Gisbert Rosen, with whom
he remained on terms of semi-sentimental friendship such as sprang up between them almost at
their first meeting in Leipzig a year earlier, and
Moritz Semmel (the brother-in-law of Robert's
eldest brother Édouard) between whom and
Robert there existed an intimate affection of a
more manly order. The contrasting quality of
these two friendships no one realized better than
did Robert himself ; he said he valued them
equally though differently, and it is fairly clear
that the responsive Robert, easily influenced, was
to each of them, exactly what each was to him.
They made a happy little fraternity, each seeing the
life about them through the roseate glasses of youth
and friendship ; but beyond this little intimate
band of three—" the three-leaved clover " he
called them—there were naturally others.

Perhaps the chief of these others was Albert Theodor Töpken, doctor of law, an enthusiastic musical amateur, whom Robert was able to help in his piano studies, and with whom he kept up a correspondence for many years after. Of his own musical activities, beyond continuing his study of the technique of the piano as inculcated by Friedrich Wieck, he most enjoyed developing his gift of improvisation.

It was arranged that at the end of the term he should spend a couple of months in Northern Italy, travelling by way of Switzerland, and in August he accordingly set out, alone this time, and crossed into Switzerland at Basle. He ascended the Rigi, and a few days later crossed the Gemmi pass into Italy. He made several acquaintances, but the fact of his travelling alone, tended to throw him back on his habit of dreamy contemplation, and to wrap him once more in his own musing which led to posing.

Of music he naturally heard a good deal, and drew the conclusion that such music was heard to best advantage beneath an Italian sky. He expressed himself, in a letter to Friedrich Wieck, as enraptured with the music of Gioachino Rossini who was then at the zenith of his fame, and whose opera *William Tell*, had just been produced in Paris.

What most appealed to him, and amazed him, was the fiery manner in which Italian orchestras played; but he was disappointed in their lack of precision and grace.

In Milan he was enchanted with the singer Giuditta Pasta, then only twenty-one, and still at the beginning of her operatic career. To Wieck he writes: "At the Gewandhaus the genius of music has sometimes filled me with fear: but in Italy I have learned to love it."

Before reaching Milan, Robert visited the Lago Maggiore, and later he saw Padua, Venice, Verona, Brescia and Vicenza.

In a letter to his sister-in-law (Moritz Semmel's handsome sister) he writes: " I always pass myself off as a Prussian here; for as the Prussian nation is the most highly thought of, it makes it easier for me. It is a sad thing to have to deny one's country but it is a good dodge."

Coming upon such a piece of surprising meanness as this, one feels inclined to apply to him Sir Toby's epithet, " a very dishonest paltry boy."

In the same letter he tells of his making good progress with his Italian; but none the less makes the usual complaint of being systematically fleeced by inn-keepers and shop-keepers.

As his journey unfolded, there were of course his invariable money bothers. He wrote in September to Gisbert Rosen that he had spent all his money and lamented that he would have to sell his watch. In another to Theodor Töpken, he wrote: " Lucky you, not to know the feeling of having to ask an inn-keeper's forbearance from week to week."

However, he cajoled a loan of sixteen gold napoleons from a confiding hotel-keeper in Milan, and cozened a tolerable sum out of his eldest brother, Edouard, finally taking Augsburg on his homeward route in order to be able to raise a loan from friend Kurrer. It is not an attractive picture.

The end of October found him in Heidelberg again, installed in fresh rooms that his friend Rosen had found for him. In his first term he had made at any rate some fleeting attempt to study law; but from this time onwards he seems to have determined that, Jurisprudence or no, music was his rightful profession, and that, in music, his rôle must be that of a pianist.

He began to practise in earnest, some seven hours a day, and at odd times used a small dumb keyboard to strengthen his fingers.

In writing to Friedrich Wieck he told him that his touch in *forte* passages had become richer, and that it was also much more full and rhythmic (schwungvoll) when playing *piano*. He crowed blithely about his being the best pianist in Heidelberg, but on one occasion only did he make a public appearance there. He chose Moscheles' Variations on the *Alexandermarsch* (for piano and orchestra) and obtained an immediate success, being frequently asked to appear again, not only in Heidelberg but at neighbouring towns.

These invitations he resolutely declined; but his fame had spread and he became something of a favourite at Heidelberg social functions, being even honoured with a pressing invitation from Grand Duchess Stephanie to visit her at the Mannheim.

Professor Thibaut included him in his weekly gatherings for the performances of Handel's Oratorio and operas, and formed a high opinion of Robert's musicianship. He seems to have tired of hearing so much of Handel's music, and in a letter to Friedrich Wieck complained of the Professor's limited outlook and pedantic single-sidedness.

An outstanding event of his year at Heidelberg was an Easter expedition by post-chaise to Frankfort, some forty miles, to hear the great Paganini play his *Caprices*. Robert had already heard Paganini in Italy, and it was doubtless his enthusiasm that spurred the party of four students to undertake the journey. The effect upon them of Paganini's playing was intensely vivid, and one of its first results was the composition of six studies, Op. III, arranged for the pianoforte after (24) Caprices of Paganini.

He became a member of one of the students' clubs, the Saxo-borussia, and entered into their various ceremonials and devilments: he also took no inactive part in the social arrangements of the town; so that with the major part of his days occupied with music, and the major part of his night occupied with the steady work of amusing himself, Jurisprudence, in so far as it was any concern of Robert Schumann, went to the wall.

In the year 1829 Robert composed the set of *Variations in the name of Abegg*, that became his Opus I, the title-page displaying a dedication to an imaginary "Mademoiselle Pauline, Comtesse d'Abegg ". The name Abegg was one well known in the neighbouring district about Mannheim and this gave an air of verisimilitude to the dedication sufficient to promote a searching inquiry from Schumann's mother as to who was the Comtesse in question.

Robert wrote a quizzical reply, and seems thoroughly to have enjoyed his little mystification. The variations are not of any great interest, and indeed are such as might have been devised by many a clever amateur well acquainted with the compositions of Moscheles and Hummel.

He succeeded in getting them published in 1832, and was furious with a critic who wrote of them as being monotonous.

Heidelberg life on his own lines suited him very well, and he wrote (March, 1830) in excellent spirits to his guardian—good as gold but as stiff as a poker—asking for his consent to staying a further six months at the University.

His guardian's consent was duly forthcoming, but probably not without some searching inquiries about his legal studies, for whether or not he was in reality doing any work in that direction at the time, we find him shortly afterwards protesting to his mother who had enquired about his piano playing, that his father would never have stood in the way of his art, and that the study of the law " freezes the flower of the imagination."

At last, in July, came the inevitable crisis. He seems at length to have grown tired of his eternal trifling with the truth ; and disgusted with the unreality of his position as a refractory law student with neither the will nor the natural gifts to make himself efficient, he seems indeed at last to have decided that, abandoning further subterfuge, he would stand forth face to face with the facts, and make an effort to start honestly upon the career of a musician which he felt to be his natural destiny.

With this determination, he wrote to his mother (July, 1830), setting out his views and aspirations in a manly way that is all too new in his correspondence : and the whole may be briefly summarized thus : " Although, guided by good intentions, and the best of good motherly reasons, you have directed me towards a legal career, I know now that if I followed the natural bend of my genius, it would lead to music," and he finishes by proposing first, that she shall consent to his abandoning, at once and for all, the study of Jurisprudence ; and, second, that she forthwith consult either Professor Thibaut of Heidelberg, or Friedrich Wieck of Leipzig, upon the question of whether or not he possessed such exceptional musical ability as would justify his

taking up music as his profession, agreeing before-
hand that he would accept their ruling.

This letter of July, 1830, written when he was
twenty years of age, was his first frank stroke for
freedom. Until then, he had done no more
than whine about his hardships ; and, swathing
his soul in an enervating poultice of self-pity, had
only whined the more when he made it too hot.

Yet there is no denying that the fact of his
musical genius having been either misunderstood,
or undervalued by his family and his guardian,
had undoubtedly made him a sufferer.

At length came the definite reaction. A
French critic, whose name escapes me, has asked
us to believe that we take pleasure in stage plays because we like to see other people suffer. This dictum
has in it a cynical sound ; but it is based none the
less on something lying very near the truth, which
I prefer to believe to be that it is not the suffering
of our fellows that we joy in seeing, but rather
the kind and degree of bravery or heroism that is
called forth to combat the misfortunes or catastrophe that befall our fellows and cause them to
suffer.

If we have sought up to now for aught in the
way of ordinary bravery, not to speak of heroism,
in the way Schumann has met his adverse fortune,
we shall have been disappointed. And how
must it have appeared to the mother ?

Recognizing at last the inevitable, though
unwillingly enough, she decided no longer to

thwart Robert's natural bent, and having come to this decision, within a week, despite the heated opposition of her three elder sons, she sent the proposed letter to Friedrich Wieck, laying the circumstances fairly before him, and asking for his candid opinion as to Robert's chances of a successful career as a pianist.

Wieck's answer, though assuring her that, with his musical talents and imagination, Robert might well become, within three years, one of the greatest living pianists, can have brought but a bitter-sweet gratification to the fond mother, for the difficulties forseen by Wieck were not concerned with the lad's musical talents, but with his unsatisfactory *character*.

He expressed the greatest concern at the instability that he had observed in him : regretted that he was not of a more manly disposition ; and asked whether he would be willing to devote a couple of years to the study of musical theory. Finally he proposed a probationary period of six months, after which he would be willing to pronounce judgment.

Both letters were sent on to Heidelberg, and Robert was in an ecstasy of excitement.

" My most honoured Master," wrote he to Wieck : " Those letters have put me in a whirl— and it has taken me a few days to arrange my ideas about them. I have read my mother's letter, and yours, *and am now much calmer* . . . I trust entirely in you, and surrender my career into your hands : take me as I am and be patient with me. I am beyond being crushed by blame, nor could any amount of praise make me lazier."

Some of this reads modestly enough, but his adoption of a rather flamboyant style in several of the other passages in the letter induce a doubt as to how far it was sincerely felt.

" Trust in me," he ends, " and I will deserve to be known as your pupil."

On the same day as that on which he sent his letter to Friedrich Wieck, he wrote to Herr Rudel, acquainting him with his acceptance of the terms that were offered him, and assuring his guardian that if at the expiration of the six months' probation, Wieck's opinion should be against him, even if he should express the smallest doubt, he would *gladly* take his examination a year later, and would have lost nothing of his Jurisprudence.

This would seem to have been exceedingly likely for obvious reasons.

After his past experience of his ward, Herr Rudel may or may not have believed this promise ; but he was apparently content to fall in with the mother's changed views.

In his usual impecunious state, Robert found himself stranded in Heidelberg some days after the end of the summer term ; but on receiving a remittance from his guardian that enabled him to settle his pressing bills, he promptly indulged himself with a trip down the Rhine, taking Mainz and all the romantic parts lying between

Rudesheim and Köningswinter ; then on through
Köln as far as Wesel. By this it was the end of
September, and high time for him to begin to
make his way towards Leipzig, so passing through
Münster and Cassel, not forgetting to spend a
few days with Gisbert Rosen's family at Detmold,
he arrived at his destination about the middle of
October, with the profession of pianist before his
eyes.

CHAPTER VI

1830—1833

Leipzig—Studies with Friedrich Wieck—Damage to hand—
—Career of composer adopted—Heinrich Dorn—*Allegro di
Bravura*—*Papillons*—Rupture with Dorn—*Six Intermezzi*—
Bach's fugues—*Symphony in G* begun—Carl Friedrich Gunther—
Julius Knorr—Henrietta Voigt—G minor piano sonata—Second
set of Paganini studies—The *Toccata* finished—Piano *Im-
promptus*—Letter to Töpken—Extract from diary—Critique
from Wiener Musikalische Zeitung—Death of Julius
Schumann—Robert's illness.

MARCUS AURELIUS ANTONINUS defined man as a
gregarious social animal; and, assuming the
truth of all that is implied in this definition, it
follows that lengthy periods of solitude are
opposed to the instincts of our healthy human
nature, as tending to induct it into channels
undesirable to its well-being.

A strong character, of the kind not easily
impressed by the sadness of solitude, will, by the
very fact of its unimpressionability, suffer less than
will one with the more emotional temperament
of the artist. But possessing the emotional
temperament in an exceptional degree, super-
imposed as it was upon the desperate seriousness
of the sentimental Saxon, Robert Schumann
was one for whom a solitary life held special
dangers.

The difference of age between his brothers and himself had sufficed, when backed by his precociously sensitive nature, to set him apart in his early boyhood from their more stodgy practicability. His school days brought him few friends, and the early loss of his father robbed him of guidance at a time when it was most needed.

Lord Byron's works had by then over-run Europe, and become the fashion. Every sentimental young man wrote his own Byronics, and adopted the picturesque pose of being wronged by all the world, and of carrying an unassuagable sorrow in his breast. If we add to this the sentimentality of Jean Paul Richter, of the debilitating stream of which Robert Schumann drank deeply, we have something of the causes of our having seen in him when he left home for Leipzig University at the age of eighteen, a self-indulgent, sentimental prig. We have seen that the latter part of his holiday in Bavaria was spent with no companion save the artificial self that he carried about with him, and he entered upon his University life in a state of morbid dissatisfaction with his lot, and of devastating self-pity.

In the following year something of the sense of the joy of living entered into him, dating from his enjoyment of the genial companionship of Wilhelm Häring; and after his Italian tour, which was unfortunately made without a companion, we have seen how in Heidelberg his nature developed in the happy fellowship of a few student friends; and, eventually, as the natural honesty within him bred more and more disgust at the unreality of his mode of living, we have seen how he decided to cast the slough of insincerity, and come into the open to demand the right of following the true bent of his genius. We have seen what signal success attended his efforts, and with what vigour he proclaimed his resolve for the future.

He had, however, overlooked the fell demon of solitude, who again attended him on his travels down the Rhine and across the country to Leipzig, with the inevitable result that he reached the University city in a state of discontent, and within a few days wrote a letter to his mother packed with petty complainings.

It is obvious that much that was ignoble remained in Robert Schumann, still to be purged away before his character was formed in the mould in which we have learned to see it through the almost infallible guide of his compositions.

Viewing the city of Leipzig as it was at the time when Schumann returned there for the purpose of studying the pianoforte with Friedrich Wieck, it was no city of romance to compare with his beloved Heidelberg. Though the town was originally built among linden trees, and although three rivers ran through it to unite a few miles away, the lie of the land was uninspiringly flat ; and though a well-built city, it was generally of a utilitarian rather than a picturesque aspect. Of the three castles it possessed in the middle ages only one remained, the Pleissenberg, and that was, either already at that time, or soon after it, turned into barracks and offices, whilst its moat had been adapted to the purposes of a drill ground.

Leipzig had always been the principal trading town of Saxony, and was the chief mart of literature for the whole of the German states ; having supported three fairs every year ever since the twelfth century. Its university, dating from the early part of the fifteenth century, had distinguished itself, in the next, by the stubbornness with which its respectability opposed the Reformation. It remained a highly respectable city, and was so when Robert Schumann took up his residence there at the age of twenty, destined to make it his home for the next fourteen years.

He had, in his last months at Heidelberg devoted much time to the study of the pianoforte ; but Friedrich Wieck's opinion was that when he left Leipzig in the spring of 1829, Robert knew far more of the technique of the instrument than when he returned eighteen months later.

Little is known of Schumann's first year after his return to Leipzig, except that he was living

alone, and working hard, if perhaps spasmo-
dically, at his piano technique ; that he was
subject to periods of exhilaration and of desperate
depression, and that he lived in a state of
perpetual financial crisis.

It is annoying to have to face so frequently
this disappointing side of Schumann's character ;
but there is far too much evidence of his habits
of begging and borrowing for it to be possible
to slur it over, and still give anything like a true
impression of the man as he then was.
Thoroughly aware, as his guardian and his mother
were, of this weakness, it seems almost incredible
that they still continued a method of providing
him with money that was only suitable to a
person either much older, or much more syste-
matic.

To send to him at Heidelberg at the outset
of a month's holiday on the Rhine, the funds
that they expected to suffice for at least several
weeks of his subsequent residence in Leipzig, seems
to have been nothing less than inviting trouble.

He was not on the best of terms with his
brothers, who had no very high opinion of him,
owing no doubt to his habitual " sponging "
upon them—and one cannot but see that such
methods as that of begging his mother *and* one
of his brothers each to send him a draft, and
begging *each* of them at the same time *not to
mention the matter to the other* must have been
rather provoking to them.

Robert arrived at Leipzig with empty pockets, and disliking having no money, promptly wrote to his mother complaining that he had spent it. He asked her to send him a hundred thalers, strengthening his request with pitiful details : he had eaten meat only twice in two weeks : was burning his last candle : and was even unable to buy himself a pistol to shoot himself.

All this may have been intentionally over-drawn, but the fact remains that he had spent his remittance and was borrowing right and left of acquaintances in Leipzig.

He was none the less working with great energy, though as Friedrich Wieck was constantly away on tours with his prodigy daughter, the instruc-tional part of it must have been undesirably intermittent.

In his exaggerated moods he could scarcely fail to give contradictory impressions of his progress, indeed, while he was capable of asserting that under Wieck's guidance he expected to become the equal of Ignaz Moscheles within four years—no sign here of the modest cough of the minor poet—he did not hesitate to change his view of his progress enough to warrant him in writing to Johann Hummel at Weimar begging to be taken as a pupil. He seems conveniently to have overlooked his promise to his mother to study with Wieck for three years ; and wrote to her in December (1830) that he intended remov-ing to Weimar to study with Hummel instead.

When Wieck heard of this project (and Robert mentioned it to him casually) he gave Robert a *mauvais quart d'heure* in his best manner. The plan was accordingly abandoned, but in his correspondence Robert harks back to the idea from time to time.

It will be remembered that while Robert was at Heidelburg University he was known to carry about with him a small dumb keyboard used for the strengthening of his fingers. His enthusiasm now led him to devise an ingenious elaboration of this apparatus, by means of which he anticipated taking a short cut towards perfect digital control. It consisted of a mechanism that, while holding up one finger of the right hand, enabled him still to practice with all the others. He had expected this would give them greater independence of action, but the result was a catastrophe. By May or June (1832) his right hand was crippled for a time, and he never regained the normal use of his third finger.

His ambition had been to become a virtuoso of the piano, and although at the time he did not anticipate the damage being permanent, the occurrence was sufficiently disturbing. Friedrich Wieck, to whom he had shown his contrivance, foreseeing the danger, had forbidden its use and was not very sympathetic, but took him to Dresden to obtain medical advice.

Robert wrote home that "a curious misfortune" had befallen him. His letter showed no sign of panic; but when, after a couple of months there was little or no improvement, he sought further advice, and underwent several different kinds of treatment, each of which, he was convinced, would prove successful. Unfortunately each was equally unsuccessful, and in November he wrote home that although his doctors still tried to re-assure him, he was satisfied that it was beyond recovery, and he had resigned himself to the inevitable.

This was a bitter blow; but he rallied from it with greater fortitude than, judging from what we have up to now seen of his character, one had reason to expect.

The blow had fallen, and although through several years he tried every cure that held the prospect of success, one is glad to recognize his pluck in facing the catastrophe. When the blow fell, he at once determined that as he could not be a performer of music he would be a composer. Strangely enough there seems to have been little or no opposition to this, though to his family the financial prospects of a composer must have seemed even more hazardous than those of a piano virtuoso.

His studies with Friedrich Wieck had, of course, to cease; but despite the maestro's rough manner, he had a genuine affection for Robert, and took him to live at his house, where they remained fellow lodgers for about a year.

Since his return to Leipzig in the autumn of 1830, Schumann had been studying composition with Heinrich Dorn, the young and enterprising director of the Leipzig Opera ; and from a letter we learn that by January 1832, he had progressed as far as the study of fugue in three parts. In April, however, his studies with Heinrich Dorn came to a sudden end ; for although he had made rapid progress, he seems to have felt himself hampered by the more plodding methods of his master which ill suited his practice of turning from one branch of the art to another without regard to his master's views as to the suitability of their sequence. As had happened in Zwickau with poor Kuntzsch, so it happened again in Leipzig : Dorn tired of what he could only regard as the waywardness of his pupil, and despite his genuine admiration for his talent, decided to teach him no more.

What appeared to Dorn as mere waywardness was, however, in reality Schumann's uncanny intuition as to what he *needed* musically, prompted by the unerring instinct of his half-awakened genius.

While studying with Dorn, and soon after his return from Heidelberg, he began the composition of a pianoforte sonata in B natural. This did not progress satisfactorily on the lines originally intended, and eventually became the *Allegro di Bravura*, Opus VIII, and was published in 1835, dedicated to the Baroness Ernestine de Fricken ; but she comes into a later story.

Schumann made several versions of this *Allegro* before he thought it fit for publication, but it was never a favourite work of his.

He also composed at this time a set of twelve piano pieces, entitled *Papillons*, that duly appeared as his Opus II. These dance movements were dedicated to his three sisters-in-law, Thérèse, Rosalie and Emilie, and were, perhaps influenced to some extent by Schumann's enthusiasm for Schubert's waltzes. Beyond their humour they contained something undeniably original and personal to Schumann himself ; and though his attempt to show them in special relation to each other was somewhat vague, he indeed admitting that the thread binding them together was scarcely visible, the circumstances surrounding their composition are none the less interesting. Schumann ascribed their genesis to his reading of Jean Paul Richter's romance, *Die Flegeljahre* —a title which Thomas Carlyle rendered into English as *Wild Oats*.

To his friend H. F. Rellstab, the editor of *Iris im Gebiete der Tonkunst*, he wrote thus :

" You recall the last scene of *Die Flegeljahre* the masked dance—Walt and the masks—Wina— Vult dancing—how the masks were exchanged— leading to the confessions, revelations, anger— the hurrying away—the conclusion and the brother's departure ? As I sat reading, and re-reading, turning again and again the last pages, I seemed to see in them, not so much an ending, as a new beginning. Then I drifted to the piano, and my little Papillons, one after another, came into being."

In a letter to Henriette Voigt, with whom he adopted a rather lighter touch, he wrote :

"I could explain the *Papillons* to you, and would, if Jean Paul had not done it so much better. When you have time, read the last chapter of his *Flegeljahre*; there you will find the whole matter from a to z, even down to the seven-league boot in F sharp minor."

We have seen that, already as an amateur, Robert Schumann had in an unusual degree, the gift of spontaneous and facile improvisation, and not only were his first works composed sitting at the piano but he continued the practice up to 1839, when he changed his views and condemned it freely.

Whether or not this method of composition had any result upon his style, it can scarcely be disputed that his style was different from any that had gone before it. In January—that is four or five months before his special exercise for the muscles of the hand proved so disastrous— Schumann sent Friedrich Wieck a letter that not only showed the growing trouble with his composition master, but also throws an interesting light upon Schumann's musical outlook at that time. Here is the passage freely translated :

" I shall never be able to get along with Dorn ; he believes that in fugue lies the whole art of music—heavens ! Nevertheless my studies with him are of real service to me. Formerly in composition I never looked beyond the inspir- ation of the moment ; but now I have learnt how to pause in the middle, so that I may look round and see just where I have arrived. I wonder whether this is what happens to you ? Many composers, such as Mozart, never do ; some like Hummel pull through; others stick fast like Schubert : and some like Beethoven can afford to laugh at it."

The above was written in January (1832), and in April Dorn threw him over; and so much to Schumann's chagrin, that he wrote an apologetic letter from which we can make significant extracts.

" I have not been idle since you deserted me. The trouble is that I seem naturally to place myself in opposition to any stimulus that comes to me from without: I want to overcome difficulties on my own initiative : . . . but I hope some day to study canon with you again . . .

" I missed your help in the arrangements for the piano that I have been making of some Paganini *Caprices* : but I saved myself by keeping them simple. I have also written six *Intermezzi* for the piano, with a prelude and fugue on three subjects in the olden style ! I should like you to see them."

In these six *Intermezzi*—published in the following year (1833) as Opus IV—one recognises a freer expression of the composer's personality than in the *Papillons*, and it is interesting to mark the first appearance in one of them of the composer's verbal guides towards interpretation, in the addition of Gretchen's line, " Meine Ruh ist hin," from Goethe's *Faust*.

Four years later (1837) Franz Liszt wrote a searching but appreciative critique of the *Intermezzi* in the *Gazette Musicale*.

Notwithstanding the conciliatory spirit of his letter to Heinrich Dorn, Schumann realized that he had from that time forward finished with instruction from others, and must henceforward study in his own way. He had always expressed a deep admiration for the works of Johann Sebastian Bach, and he now took to the serious study of them. He wrote to his old professor, Johann Kuntzsch, in Zwickau, that he found Bach's *Wohltemperirte Klavier* the best studies for him and that he had made complete analyses of all the fugues. In the same letter, July (1832) he informed Kuntzsch that he intended taking up the study of instrumentation, and in November of the same year he asked the conductor of the Euterpe concerts at Leipzig, Gottlieb Müller, to oblige him by going through a symphonic movement that he had composed and which was shortly to be produced. He added that his orchestration was carried out entirely according to his own ideas; but that he was somewhat uncertain of his ability in regard to symphonic writing.

It is not known whether Müller gave him any advice about instrumentation, or whether he ever saw this work, which was the first movement of a symphony in G. The movement was duly performed at Zwickau on 18th November (1832) but the success of the concert was not Schumann's symphonic movement, but the piano-playing of little Clara Wieck, then thirteen years of age, whose performance took the audience by storm. This was the first time that Schumann had had an opportunity of hearing the realization of his orchestral ideas. It is an illuminating experience for any composer; but in spite of the work not being well received, Schumann was lucky enough to be invited by the conductor at the neighbouring town of Schneeburg, to allow him to repeat it the following January. He at once set to work to remedy such defects as he could, and the same movement with probably the addition of others, was given in Leipzig in June, 1833, and was more favourably received, Schumann saying that it made him a good many friends among musicians.

He spent the winter of 1832-33 at Zwickau with his mother, and at Schneeburg with one of his brothers; and on his return to Leipzig in the spring he went to live with Carl Friedrich Gunther, a musician of no outstanding merit.

Another friend of this time was Julius Knorr, half musician, half literary man. It is interesting to observe that more of Schumann's friends were literary rather than musical; writing came easily to him, and he contributed occasional articles at this time to the *Leipziger Tageblatt*, the *Allgemeine Musikalische Zeitung*, and to *Der Komet*, a critical magazine edited by Georg Herlossohn. Herlossohn was also a friend of his, and one of the little circle that met nightly for supper at a chosen restaurant, when they consumed great quantities of beer as was the general custom of the time.

Since Robert's patrimony had been handed over, he was in fairly easy circumstances. His capital was invested, and his income generally sufficed for his needs as a bachelor, indeed, he was able to offer assistance to one of his brothers on more than one occasion.

Some idea of how he passed his time is to be obtained from his own description: " The morning Italian: the evening Dutch. Up by five o'clock: out of bed like a young roe: then letters and the diary: work at music till eleven, when friend Luke arrives: dinner at noon: read French until three: then a three hours' ramble, more often alone than not: more music until eight when it is time to join my friends at the *Kaffeebaum* for supper."

One receives an impression of a twist in the mind that led him to a preference for being alone:

or is it at this time only a mood remaining with him from the days of his spurious Byronics ? Though a facile writer he was no talker ; even at supper with his coterie he generally preferred to sit silent ; while at the Wieck's music-parties where he was a frequent guest his hostess informed Professor Niecks that Robert " generally sat quietly in a corner swinging one foot." This picture gives one the impression of a shy boy with no manners ; and a little incident related by Henriette Voigt, a young married woman with whom he was on terms of sentimental friendship, certainly indicates an unusual turn of mind :

" One summer evening, after making music together, we went on the river in a boat. After a complete silence of an hour's duration, Robert pressed my hand tenderly, saying, ' And now we perfectly understand each other.' "

Musically he was industrious ; busy with his studies, busy with composition, continuing the work upon his *Symphony in G*, which he completed by April 1833, and also essaying a pianoforte concerto. He composed two movements of a pianoforte *sonato in G minor*, upon which he worked from time to time throughout the succeeding five years, publishing it in 1839 as Opus 22 ; and also began work upon the F sharp minor sonata (Op. 11).

Professor Niecks suggests that this was the work

to which Schumann referred in writing to his mother at the end of January (1831).

" My holiday was so quiet that I really neither spoke nor heard a sound. I sank into a kind of lethargy that for some years past seizes me at times—then I started on a gigantic work, which requires my whole strength, and at this moment I am more fresh and healthy and proud than I can tell you."

He followed up his first set of piano pieces founded on Paganini violin *Caprices*, by a second set (Opus X) and in these he allowed himself a greater freedom than in the previous set, although we know that in this task he told Dorn that he missed his guiding hand. He sent the work, however, to Friedrich Wieck, and with refreshing modesty begged him to "sit down by Clara, as she plays them, and mark in pencil anything that occurs to you."

He next turned to the *Toccata* that he had begun in Heidelberg in 1830 and left unfinished. He found the task a difficult one, largely no doubt owing to the character of the work, a show-piece and something quite foreign to the poetic trend of his genius, it being designed as virtuoso music. " Composing progresses quickly and easily," he wrote to his favourite brother Julius, " but the after-working on my improvisations drives me to despair." The *Toccata* was published in 1834—Opus VII.

In the summer of 1833, he took a Romance by

Clara Wieck (that she, at the age of fourteen had dedicated to him) as the basis for his *Impromptus for Piano* (Op. 5). These *Impromptus* show something of the real Schumann, and lifted his work into a higher plane than that of the *Papillons* or the *Paganini Studies*. He was unable, however, to find a publisher for them on the customary basis, but as he was determined on publication he agreed to bear the cost of engraving, etc.

An intimate letter to Theodor Töpken, his Heidelberg friend, written in April of the same year, gives one a vivid impression of the composer at the age of twenty-three; it is included in F. G. Jansen's second collection of the Schumann letters, and the following is a free translation:

" My dear kind Töpken,

" Your letter, a month old, gave me great pleasure, though it scarcely came to me on eagle's wings. It reached me at home with my family, among the Erzgebirge, amid festivities that made it impossible to write with anything approaching historical calm. Do not expect very much of it even now—for, after all, a grasp of the hand is better than a ream of writing—although after all these years there is much to tell you.

" You may believe me when I say that I have often thought of you; and even in my musical dreaming there is a face in the background very much like yours. In music, and in other things, I have tried to get on to the straight road, the firm road, that you always wanted me to take. You, yourself, have taken it, and I have a great idea of your progress.

"We were all at sea in trying to take a short cut, by means of mechanical devices, to an end that can only be gained by persistent toil through the years : in fact, we gripped the handle so strongly that we almost broke the beaker—but the reverse would have been even worse. I have had too good cause to change my views, and I have set aside as mere hindrances many things that I once deemed infallible. Only by keeping the development of one's mechanical dexterity in step with one's mental capacity, can one hope for artistic perfection. I try to express myself precisely, but could explain myself better if we could talk it over together. If you have my first set of studies after Paganini's violin caprices you will find what I am now trying to explain put much better than I am expressing it here.

"So you know my *Papillons*. I am glad, for many of the ideas came to me when we were together in Heidelberg. For one thing they showed you I was still alive, and I shall value your criticism. There was a review in a Vienna paper that pleased me much, and something flattering, too, in the Berlin *Iris*.

"Two books of *Intermezzi* will be published after Easter ; (they are really extended *Papillons* and an *Allegro di bravura*), and I will let you know when they appear.

✦ "All last winter I was working at a great symphony for orchestra ; and without wishing to be conceited, I expect great things from it.

"I scarcely play the piano these days : don't be amazed : I crippled one of the fingers of my right hand : but I am quite resigned : indeed it seems almost Providential now. It began by being only a slight injury ; but owing to careless treatment I can now scarcely play at all. When I write again I will tell you all about it, and tell you about my prospects ; they look very rosy at present. I will tell you too how I have been received in the artistic world—nothing could be more encouraging and I am full of plans for the future. My daily life here is very orderly and staid in comparison with our Bohemian ways in Heidelberg : but I am working hard too.

"When writing you had best address me to care of Wieck who is now my best friend here. You will have read about his daughter Clara : imagine everything that is most perfect, and I will endorse it all. Moscheles was simply amazed at her playing.

"I am in correspondence with Hummel, and if you are interested I will tell you his opinions of me—you would find them very like your own.

"It is just a year ago to-day that our merry

party in the one-horse carriage set out for Frankfort to hear Paganini. Here are some jottings from my diary :

" ' Our first coachman—cloudy sky—the rough mountain road—the Melibocus—Auerbach —Benecke—I just caught him stepping into the coach for Berlin—the little waitress—Lichtenberg's bill of sale—and laughter—Forster—the Malaga—then Schädler and Eckmayer pledging each other in bumpers—collisions in the passage, etc.'

" ' *Easter Sunday.* Töpken's terrible language— Downcast faces—Darmstadt—Pretty weeping-willow in the inn court-yard—April weather, all blue and black—the Frankfort watch-tower— the lame horse and how we had to run beside it— We reach the Swan—In the evening Paganini— Wasn't it rapturous ?—Weber (he never wrote to me afterwards !), Hille and you at the Swan—Music in the distance, and bliss on going to bed.

" ' *Easter Monday.* The charming girl of the Willow Bush—Rossini's *William Tell* in the evening—Töpken's excellent judgment—our rush to reach the Willow Bush—the pretty girl and our opera glass contest—champagne.

" ' *Easter Tuesday.* Piano with Töpken—Al. Schmitt—Schubert's Waltzes—Braunfels—Waxworks—Weber leaves (up to now it has been good-bye for ever !)—We leave Frankfort—My ingenious digression into slums—Darmstadt—

Delicious feeling after a pint of wine—Töpken rather full—The Melibocus bathed in evening light—full of wine—our miserable steed—our new coachman—arrived at Auerbach—Little Lottie—My dispute with Töpken—Lose my temper for the first time for years.

"'*Easter Wednesday*. Rain—the wonderful blossoms along the mountain road—Handschuchsheim and the miserable Prussian foxes—Home again.'

"I cannot remember ever having enjoyed copying anything so much as this, excepting, of course, my own music; for it has brought you most livingly into my mind. I could almost write you an even longer letter than this for the sole purpose of letting you know how much I have always loved and respected you : *always*, excepting on that one night at Auerbach, when no cannon balls would have damaged us so much as the volleys of grape that we indulged in— really that small-shot hurts one to the very bones. But it was amusing *afterwards*, and you have so often pardoned me my share of the adventure that I need not ask you to do so again.

"The best of greetings in all friendship ! May you soon be able to disperse the clouds that have overhung the last two years : perhaps they will turn to warm drops, and fall upon the hand of your friend,

"R. Schumann.

" Here is the critique at full length from the *Wiener Musikalische Zeitung* :

1. Theme sur le nom, etc.

2. Papillons.

" It is always a pleasure to stand upon one's own legs, needing neither a crutch, nor the arm of a friend. The name of the composer is new to us, he is probably young, but (here I was both startled and excited) is one of the rarities of our day. He is the follower of no school of composition, but seeks his inspiration entirely within himself (that's how I come to drink so little nowadays) without striving for extraneous decoration. Quite otherwise: for he has dreamed a new world to revel in, and cuts his capers with originality and sometimes with eccentricity too. Being at heart a phœnix, he is none the less worthy of the *accolade*—(look it up in the dictionary).

" Such people as those for whom Jean Paul's intensely subtle pictures of life are caviare, and those for whom Beethoven's flashes of genius are an emetic, will probably feel no less scandalized here ; but will sneer at the temerity of a composer, quite unknown, and make a great noise in decrying his music. They may even spoil a few quires of paper, and a couple of dozen quills in explaining how this *ought* to have been written. Well, let them ! Music that is published must be prepared for all kinds of public opinion : and only a conceited composer will despise it. One who aspires to high things will receive them gratefully, though he will not be easily led away from the genius of his inspiration.

" And now a few words about the two compositions. The first is founded upon a group of five notes, *a*, *b*, *e*, *g*, *g*, : (were you surprised at my Gräfin Pauline ? I am her sole progenitor, and will explain the mystification to you later : I had my reasons). The second, after half-a-dozen bars of introduction, consists of twelve fantastic phrases, of different length, different key, different time and different rhythm, generally vivacious, capricious suggestions of butterfly nature. (They were meant by me to suggest something altogether different from that ; and I will give you the clue to the idea in my next letter.) They are by no means easy to play, requiring as they do carefully characterized interpretation, and needing considerable study."

" I nearly fell asleep in copying out all this, as you can see from my writing. But my industry will be amply rewarded if you will send me your answer soon, telling me, too, about your own musical studies in which I am always deeply interested. Let me recommend my Paganini Caprices as useful studies, and let me have your opinion on them. I learn that the writer of the critique in the Vienna paper was Grillparzer the poet."

The foregoing is one of the first critiques, or at any rate one of the first inseeing critiques of Schumann's music: and the value that he attached to it is obvious by his taking the trouble to copy it out for Töpken. It was certainly an event in his artistic career of sufficient importance to make the reproduction of the article desirable here. His works published at this period (1832-33) were generally speaking fairly well received in the press, though with no outstanding enthusiasm but they were welcomed by musicians of note who did not hesitate to send him generous letters of congratulation. One of them, Johann Nepomuk Hummel, a great power in his day, warned him, as a friend, against allowing his adoption of sudden changes of harmony in quick succession to become a mannerism, as in his opinion it would destroy the charm and beauty of his compositions. It will be remembered that in the summer of 1831, Schumann had asked Hummel to take him as a piano pupil, but though they were not personally known to each other it is clear that the older man (he was then fifty-three) regarded the youthful Schumann as a promising composer.

Towards the end of this year (1833) Julius Schumann, Robert's favourite brother, and the one nearest to his own age, fell ill, seriously. His mother urged Robert to return home to be with him, and eventually wrote with such angry energy as to extort from him a letter protesting that his own ill-health made it impossible for him to travel to her. This is the first time we have heard of his being in such ill-health, yet this is how he wrote :

" Had you the least idea of my agonizing illness you would not continue to urge me to come. If I were well I should have set out at a word from you ; but I should have thought my last refusal would have shown you that all was not well with me. I suffer from constant attacks that have kept me within doors for the last fortnight ; and am not even allowed to wash myself. If I travelled now, I should probably be carried straight from the post-chaise to my death-bed."

This seems to indicate that he was subject to the same distressing disease of the skin as that with which his sister Emilie had been afflicted. In her case it had led to acute attacks of melancholia, and the spirit of this letter obviously indicates a similar condition with Robert.

Within a few weeks of this letter Julius died, and at almost the same time his sister-in-law, Rosalie (Carl's wife). This double blow completely prostrated Robert, both physically and mentally. He could no longer bear to sleep alone, and wrote to his mother that he dared not make the journey to Zwickau, fearing that some catastrophe might befall him.

" Violent rushes of blood," he wrote to his mother in November, " unspeakable fear, breathlessness, momentary unconsciousness, alternate quickly, although less now than in the last few days. You would certainly forgive my not having written if you had the least idea of this deep-seated soul-sleep that melancholy has brought upon me."[1]

It is a disagreeable task to read Schumann's letters at this time ; for while sympathizing with his ill-health one cannot but recognize in them his selfish neglect to take any steps to help his mother in her distress, displaying thereby the complete lack of the moral stamina that would have led him to be of real service. No doubt he was completely prostrated when the blow fell ; but where was his place ? Certainly not in Leipzig.

[1] Professor Nieck's Supplementary and Corrective Biography.

Chapter VII

1834—1835

LEIPZIG

Ludwig Schunke—Henriette and Carl Voigt—Ernestine von Fricken—The Kaffeebaum group—The *Neue Zeitschrift für Musik*—Death of Schunke—*Carnaval*—*Symphonic variations*— *Piano Sonata in F ♯ minor.*

SCHUMANN's most intimate friend in the year 1834 was Ludwig Schunke, a young composer and pianist of the same age as himself, only recently arrived in Leipzig from Vienna. They lived in the same house, and immediately became close friends. Schunke was a consumptive, and in this misfortune his steadfast character and pluck showed to great advantage, constantly evoking Robert's admiration. He pictured his friend in a letter as resembling Thorwaldsen's statue of Schiller, adding a humorous reservation that the statue was really " more *Schilleresque* than Schiller ever was."

At Friedrich Wieck's house Schunke met a wealthy musical amateur, Carl Voigt, and his wife, Henriette who has already been mentioned. To these enthusiasts Schumann was introduced by his friend, Schunke, and he soon became equally intimate with them. With Henriette Voigt, indeed, his friendship took the sentimental turn that seems to have come naturally to him, and his letters to her were frequently elaborated to the point of insufferable affectation. The episode in the boat with her will not have been forgotten, and with that in mind, this reads queerly :

" The way in which I have sometimes welcomed and sometimes repelled your expressions of sympathy, must seem such a problem of polar attraction and repulsion, that I want to show myself to you in a better light."

His letter, however, makes no attempt to do anything of the kind.

About the same time, the daughter of a wealthy Bohemian, Baron von Fricken, came to reside with the Wiecks as a pupil : Robert met her and at once fell in love with her. For him Ernestine had the head of a Madonna, and the " tender and pure soul of a child," " extraordinarily musical, and attached to him and to everything artistic." A mutual friend described Ernestine as " physically luxuriant, strongly developed on the emotional side, but intellectually insignificant."

They were very soon engaged to be married, and as Robert dearly loved a mystery, the engagement was to be kept a secret from the Wiecks, and all other friends, including, of course, Frau Henriette. It was not long ere this good lady interpreted the position correctly, but Schumann cajoled her into assisting them in carrying on a clandestine correspondence. He wrote to Henriette :

"What one wants to avoid is the awkward corner that everybody can see. I knew you realized that it was Ernestine who felt compelled to hold a veil between you and me; but you have raised it so gently, that I may now be allowed to press the hand of a friend behind it, particularly as any other would have been withdrawn in such discouraging circumstances."

Some little has been written from time to time regarding Schumann's love for Ernestine, the bosom friend of Clara Wieck, in view of his supposed preoccupation at the time with the little pianist. But in spite of his undoubted admiration for Clara, as shown by his references to her in his letters, it seems rather preposterous to attribute to him any warmer feeling towards a little girl of something less than fifteen. It is scarcely the triangle Clara—Robert—Ernestine— that intrigues one, but the other triangle Ernestine —Robert—Henriette. Let me make a short extract from another of his letters to Henriette.

"Your letter touched me like the hand of an angel. What a day and night! And then this morning, with every nerve a tear! I cried like a child over Ernestine's words written on the corner, and when I read her other notes to you, my strength gave way. Is it weak of me to own this? It is my Ernestine whom I love immeasurably, and you, too, Henriette, my beloved friend."

But Henriette was not invariably quite so tractable :

"There was a thunderstorm on your brow yesterday, and its lightnings were aimed at me. In some ways I have no excuse to make."

Robert seems to have allowed his impression-ability to run away with him, and in the light of his letters, the three of them made a curious triangle, with the husband and Ludwig Schunke well outside the figure.

The engagement lasted about a year, when mutual discoveries of unsuitability brought it to an ignominious end.

And now we can turn to another and more stable side of Robert Schumann's life at this time, —its literary side. We have already seen him sending articles on musical subjects to various papers, and associating at least as much with authors as with musicians.

At the *Kaffeebaum*, where the little group of friends spent their evenings, the talk ran gener-ally in artistic channels ; and, as is not unusual among artists, the unsatisfactory state of criticism in matters of art came up for frequent judgment and invariable condemnation. There are few subjects more apt to raise the artistic temperature than the unreasonable views of other people upon us and our work, in contrast to *our* logical and correct views upon them— or upon ourselves.

On one of the flood tides of enthusiasms was mooted the idea of starting a new and better musical paper. The idea was considered nothing less than an inspiration. But there were level heads among the enthusiasts, and nothing was to be done precipitately : it was to be the protest of youth against the existing state of things in art, and surrounding art, summarized in one word —superficiality.

Almost the only musical paper of any standing in Germany of that day was the *Allgemeine musikalische Zeitung*, the name of whose conservative editor to this set of enthusiasts was nothing less than Anathema Maranatha.

The field, therefore, lay open to them with its alluring possibilities of making their good influence felt among the German speaking peoples, with the added possibility of who knows what rewards in the future, for none of them was mad enough to imagine they had only to sow a few musical articles to reap an immediate golden harvest.

Little reason as Schumann had to complain personally of harsh treatment at the hands of the critics, he regarded the critical spirit of the day as the extreme antithesis of what should be the spirit of the receptive musician : and he welcomed the opportunity of demonstrating in the newspaper how much more vivid was the effect of music upon him, than upon the critics of the day, as shown by their writings.

The decision to establish a musical paper was made in May or June, 1833, and by the end of the latter month a publisher had been found, one

C. H. F. Hartmann, a bookseller. The name of the paper was decided upon, the *Neue Leipziger Zeitschrift für Musik, edited by a group of artists and amateurs :* its first directors, Robert Schumann, Friedrich Wieck, Kapellmeister Stegmayer, Ludwig Schunke, and Julius Knorr.

Ernst Ortlepp, poet and journalist, drew up a promising prospectus :

" The day of reciprocating compliments in criticism is dead and buried ; We shall never disinter it. If we feared to attack what is bad, we should be only poor supporters of what is good, etc., etc."

By the following March everything was ready. Schumann was to be editor (though his name was not mentioned), with a salary of a hundred and fifty thalers. In the event of there being insufficient profits Schumann agreed to waive his remuneration, as did several of his friends who were to contribute to the paper, notably Wieck, Knorr and Ortlepp. A Shakespearean quotation was taken from Henry VIII, and used as a motto for the paper :

> " only they
> Who come to hear a merry bawdy play,
> A noise of targets, or to see a fellow
> In a long motley coat guarded with yellow,
> Will be deceived."

The first number was published on 3rd April, 1834, and was followed by the issue of two numbers a week up to the end of the year, when Schumann became the sole proprietor, changed the publisher and openly announced himself as editor.

The list of contributors to the *Neue Zeitschrift für Musik* during the ten years of Schumann's editorship, contains many names of distinction, including that of Richard Wagner: but he was not invariably successful in his invitations to friends to write for him.

When Felix Mendelssohn was conductor at Düsseldorf, Schumann invited him either to write upon the state of music in that city, or to ask his poet friend Immermann to contribute the article. Mendelssohn's answer was characteristic of his dislike to all writing about music: " Immermann is the last man in the world to write your article, for he dislikes music; I am *the last man but one* for it, for if I managed to write anything coherent about it, the mere thought of its appearing in print would make me destroy it . . ."

Nor did his regular contributors invariably live up to his expectations. Thus, we find him writing to friend Töpken, who had become the Bremen correspondent: " If you keep us any longer in suspense about your article I shall have to make formal announcement of your death in next week's issue."

But the most important contributions were those of the editor who appeared in many guises;

for, recognising the advantage to his paper of articles written from as many different points of view as possible, and realizing that his friends were little capable of writing except from the single standpoint of their own personality, he developed the idea of the *Davidsbündler*, an imaginary brotherhood of young Davidites, all capable of taking part in the slaughter of the Philistines in imaginary discussions.

He endowed them with names and characters, the two principals of whom being *Florestan*, the downright, and *Eusebius*, the poet ; with *Master Raro* as intermediary between the two.

At a later date Schumann explained that while the majority of the Davidsbündler consisted of the imaginary persons that he had invented, and of others no less real to him, that he had borrowed from Jean Paul Richter, there were a few who represented real people, with whose views he was familiar ; thus *Jeanquirit* represented Stephen Heller ; *Jonathan* was Ludwig Schunke ; *Julius* Julius Knorr ; *Felix Meritis*, Mendelssohn ; and *Chiara*, Clara Wieck. Something of the fantasy and humour of the idea may be indicated by the following excerpt from a Shrove Tuesday address of *Florestan* :

" It is the aim of the David-brotherhood to dam the stream of mediocrity by word and by deed . . ."

" Springing onto the top of the grand piano, *Florestan* addresses his comrades in this fashion :

" Davidites here assembled : you whose destiny
it is to slay the Philistines who are all round
us, musical or otherwise, attacking the biggest
first, etc., etc."

To Schumann these fantastic people of his own
creation became very real, and he was able to
play off one against another in very lively
fashion—so that he was guilty of no exaggeration
when he wrote that in this multiplicity of
imaginary personalities he was " living a romance
unlike any that had been lived before." The novel
tone of the paper, with its humour and its
enthusiasm, soon made it popular, and its circulation rapidly increasing, its influence on musical
art in Germany became one of undeniable
importance.

In taking up this literary work it must not be
supposed that Schumann's aim was to force
upon his readers any particular beliefs of his
concerning the value of his own compositions—for,
indeed, the composer Schumann was a very
different person from the writer Schumann, though
in the style of each of them we can find something
of Friedrich von Hardenberg's " art of surprising
in a pleasing way."

Schumann was not the first composer to possess
literary gifts ; for Carl Maria von Weber and
Hector Berlioz are examples that at once occur to
mind ; but it is interesting to compare his
rhapsodical style of writing with the philosophical
style of Richard Wagner's prose works. For

Schumann a critique was not so much analytical examination or summing up, as his pæan of joy in the music he had heard and loved, and loved to write about, so that others might be brought to love it too. His pen was incredibly active; and his literary side, fostered in his boyhood by his father, and developed later under the influence of the works of his favourite romantic writers, had a far reaching effect upon his musical side. It is often held that had he given less of himself in his writings, his compositions would have expressed more: that can, of course, remain nothing more than a conjecture, and we must leave it at that. Schumann felt strongly that he had thoughts about music that had not been expressed before, and believed no less strongly that the uttering of them, and the circulation of them to the widest possible public, would react upon the progress of the art of music in Germany, an art founded upon the romantic tradition of Beethoven and Schubert, to which he wished to link something of the preceding century, probably something derived from Johann Sebastian Bach.

For Schumann, the musical critic was to be a responsive musician, quick to understand and to interpret to others. Such a view lent itself to his naturally rhapsodical style of writing; and as there was within him a genuine poetic impulse that coloured at once his outlook and his mode of expression, his articles attracted wider notice than the normal critiques of the day, and aroused a greater degree of interest.

Here was a man with a vision of something new that was coming into music. " I can perceive," wrote he, " a rose-red light, creeping upward in the sky : whence it comes who shall say ? But let us who are young make for the light."

Among the first contributors to the *Neue Zeitschrift für Musik*, was Schumann's friend, Ludwig Schunke ; but as the year 1834 drew towards its close, his health became alarmingly worse, and the rapid strides of consumption became more and more visible. Throughout the period of his residence in Leipzig he had lived under sentence of death ; but his was a genial character not easily cast down, and he made a gallant fight. To his Leipzig friends the end had been only too obvious from the first, and as his exhaustion became more constant and ever more painful, Schumann found it too distressing for him to witness, so instead of staying with his friend in the hour of his need, he packed up, deserted him, and fled to Zwickau. In the middle of October he wrote to his mother : " I am only waiting for a good day for my journey . . . . I foresee fits of melancholy, all the worse for being absent from Ernestine ; but I thank heaven for my having the strength to tear myself away from here."

From his home in Zwickau he wrote to

Henriette Voigt : " Alas, how can I endure the thought of losing him ? When he dies, let it not be you that writes it to me ; find some other hand to do that."

This pusillanimous running away from a painful duty, with no regard to the hurt he caused to his friend by so doing, is unfortunately not the sole instance of the kind ; and it no doubt arose from a supersensibility to pain that none but a more virile character would have been able to combat. Here is an excerpt from a letter to his mother (January, 1834) that shows the same shrinking from another's grief :

" I have read your letter again. . . . Nowadays the mere thought of the suffering of other people is more than I can bear, and leaves me devoid of energy. Do be careful to keep from me any news that could in the least disturb me, or I shall be compelled to put away all your letters unread. On no account remind me of anything connected with Julius or Rosalie."

So poor Schunke was left to his fate, to die, tended to the last by his friends Henriette and Carl Voigt.

It might not unreasonably be imagined that with the *Neue Zeitschrift für Musik* to be piloted through its early stages, with some degree of ill-health to contend with, with a sick friend on his hands, and with the complications arising from his various indiscretions to occupy him, Schumann would have had but little time available for serious musical composition. Yet in these years 1834-5, he composed for the piano, *Carnaval*, the *Symphonic Variations*, and completed the *Sonata in F sharp minor*, that he had begun two years before.

The *Carnaval*, (Opus 9) *Scenes mignonnes composées pour le pianoforte sur quatre notes*, was not published till 1837. It consists of twenty-one numbers, including many dance movements, each of which is provided with a suitable title. Some of these titles are simply names, such as *Chiarina* (Clara), *Estrella* (Ernestine), *Chopin* and *Paganini*; but the majority suggest the assumed characters that people a masked ball; such as *Pierrot, Arlequin, Pantalon ¡et Columbine.*

Others, such as *Aveu*, or *Coquette*, countered by its fellow, *Réplique*, are more suggestive of moods than of people; and knowing the manner of their composition, and knowing that Schumann wrote that it was only the various moods depicted in them that interested him, it is surprising to learn from his own letters that it was not until *after* their composition that he fitted them with their superscriptions : though this can scarcely apply to the last number, the *Marche des Davids bündler contre les Philistins*, which forms the climax to the whole.

There is yet another side to this composition, but one of little more than technical interest ; he had, indeed, at one time the idea of naming the work *Frolics on four notes*, owing to his having used the succession of four notes, A, E flat, C, B flat, as the basis for the whole composition.

The ingenuity is beyond question, but it is to-day unnecessary to worry about linking of the town of Asch in Bohemia, with the recurrence of its four letters in the name *Sch*um*a*nn. It is only another case of the ingenious mystification that appealed to one side of the composer's Saxon sense of humour.

Similarly, at a later date Schumann made a musical phrase from the name of the composer Gade : but irrespective of any such ingenuity, each number of *Carnaval* is complete in itself, presenting a distinctive mood in a distinctive way.

Schumann was averse to the idea of the performance at a concert of the work as a whole, feeling that as a whole it had little coherence. Pianists have thought otherwise ; but it is a matter of opinion how far their view has been influenced by their pleasure in overcoming technical difficulties, and by the fascination of the kaleidoscopic changes of colour and of mood in the successive contrasted movements.

The *Etudes Symphoniques* (Opus 13), being twelve studies in the form of variations, were published in 1837, three years after their composition.

To the pianist they present many interesting problems of technique, and the characteristic rhythms, and exuberant vitality of the music, especially of the *finale*, have made the work exceedingly popular.

These variations came into being owing to the father of Ernestine von Fricken having sent Schumann a theme and variations that he had composed for flute and piano, asking him for his opinion of the work. Schumann discovered in the amateur's work many faults of commission and omission, but finding the subject suggestive, and to his liking, set about to show how the treatment could be improved.

So interesting did the task become, that he took the subject seriously in hand, and nothing more was heard of his friend's little work for flute and piano.

The *piano Sonata in F sharp minor*, Opus 11, " composed by Florestan and Eusebius," was begun in 1833, and when completed in 1835, was dedicated to Ignaz Moscheles.

The dedication was not altogether a happy one, for when the work was played for his benefit by Clara Wieck, the great virtuoso found it " very laboured, difficult and somewhat intricate, though interesting in spite of that." Franz Liszt, however, wrote a sympathetic appreciation of the sonata, finding in it both novelty and individuality.

" The aria is one of the most perfect things that I know," wrote he. " The music will appeal to those given to meditation, and those who will take the trouble to dive for hidden pearls." His sole reservation was that some indication of the poetic import of the work would have been welcome.

Schumann's own view of the work was that it contained " much of his heart's blood," and he induced Moscheles to write about it for publication, but the article was written rather unwillingly and faintheartedly.

Schumann's artistic position — Mendelssohn — Ferdinand David — Chopin — Sterndale Bennett — Hirschbach — Niels Gade—Ferdinand Hiller—Madame Devrient—*Piano sonata in F♯ minor—Fantasie for piano—Die Davidsbündler Tänze*—Clara Wieck—The betrothal—*Fantasiestücke for piano—In der Nacht.*

ALTHOUGH the music that Schumann composed up to the age of twenty-five included several of the works that have since come to be included amongst the most successful of his pianoforte compositions, the large majority of musicians, composers and executants alike, regarded his music with suspicion, and even dislike. A small coterie of friends, and of musicians, either professional or amateur, acclaimed him, as did his literary friends. Most of the German critics (always excepting G. W. Fink, of the *Allegemeine Musikalische Zeitung,* who ignored his existence) welcomed his attitude ; but such representative musicians as Ignaz Moscheles, Felix Mendelssohn, Moritz Hauptmann of Dresden, and Louis Spohr, showed little appreciation of what he was doing.

Mendelssohn found " much that was awkward " in his music, and Hauptmann wrote of his compositions as pretty trifles, curious, but lacking solidity.

His *Neue Zeitschrift für Musik* was gradually extending the influence of his ideas, but at any rate in its first years, it was not used to advertise his music, and Schumann's love of writing under assumed names was naturally not a plan that tended to make his own name more widely known. His dictum was : anything with mystery attached to it has special power ; and with that conviction he was satisfied.

In 1835 a new influence came into Schumann's life ; and that was Felix Mendelssohn-Bartholdy. Though born only a year before Schumann, Mendelssohn was already recognized as a master. He had already composed his *Midsummer Night's Dream* music, *St. Paul*, *The Hebrides* Overture, and other orchestral works, and his appointment in 1835 to the conductorship of the Leipzig Gewandhaus concerts was an important event not only in his own life, but also in the musical life of Leipzig.

For two years before coming to Leipzig, Mendelssohn had been the musical director at Düsseldorf ; and when he came to take up his new appointment as *Capellmeister*, it signalled the arrival of a mode of orchestral conducting altogether new to Leipzig. Until that time the leading of the whole orchestra was in the hands of the leader of the first violins, who indicated what was wanted either by the demonstrative emphasis of his own bowing or by beating the time with his bow.

Following a lead given by Louis Spohr, fifteen years before, Mendelssohn came to Leipzig as "conductor" as we now know him, full of a determination to improve the performances. The plan of his artistic life, however, did not limit his activities to the direction of his orchestra ; for he looked forward to having time not only for composition, but also for painting, an art in which he was deeply interested, and to which he frequently attributed his inspirations. He was something of an *enfant gâté*, and exceedingly sensitive to adverse criticism : the slightest coolness in praising a composition was regarded as open hostility ; but as Schumann was of his admirers one of the most devoted, the two no sooner met, than they became intimate friends and formed a habit of lunching together daily. Their first meeting was at a party given by Friedrich Wieck on the eve of Mendelssohn's first Gewandhaus concert (October, 1835).

The difference in the outlook of the two friends is worthy of note ; for against writers, and particularly against writers on music, Mendelssohn cherished a strong prejudice ; and it is a tribute to both men that the fact of Schumann writing so much on music formed no stumbling block to the ripening of their friendship.

When the friendship had lasted for a couple of years, Schumann wrote to Clara Wieck : "Mendelssohn is the most distinguished man I have ever met. People say he is not really my friend ; but I don't believe it, for I know I am absolutely loyal to him. I know, too, just how I stand with him musically : for years I could go on learning from him ; and he has something to learn from me too. If only I had had his advantages I should have outsoared everybody, the energy of my ideas assures me of this."

As a composer Mendelssohn seldom appreciated Schumann's attitude, regarding him at first as a mere musical *dilettante* : and even much later, when he came to understand him better, Madame Schumann instanced the pianoforte concerto, and the second symphony as works of which Mendelssohn had no real appreciation.

As Mendelssohn's success in Leipzig became known throughout the musical world, musicians of all kinds visited the city in ever increasing numbers : and Schumann, as Mendelssohn's intimate, increased his circle of musician-friends. Among them were Ferdinand David, whom Mendelssohn brought there as his first violinist, and Ignaz Moscheles who came to give a concert a few days after Mendelssohn's first Gewandhaus appearance ; François Frederic Chopin made a flying visit in September (1835), and was enchanted with Clara Wieck's interpretation of the last movement of his pianoforte concerto, and some of his études. She also played for him Schumann's *F♯ minor sonata*, and, by way of return, Chopin played for her one of his own nocturnes, in which, by the way, Clara thought his playing "altogether too capricious."

This was Schumann's first meeting with Chopin, for whose music he had a sincere respect if not a deep affection.

Another who came on a first visit of eight months was William Sterndale Bennett, who became the intimate friend of both Mendelssohn and Schumann, the latter of whom impressed him as "one of the finest hearted men he had ever known."

We hear of Hermann Hirschbach, whose music made a profound impression upon Schumann, his string quartets appearing to Schumann as "the most colossal to be met with to-day. A passionate, tragic writer; original both as to form and as to treatment; some parts moved me most deeply: an overwhelming imagination."

Niels Gade came from Copenhagen, and if one may draw a conclusion from his compositions, his pilgrimage was by no means fruitless.

Ferdinand Hiller, the pupil of Hummel whom Schumann had approached in 1831, came to Leipzig at Mendelssohn's invitation to superintend the production of his oratorio *Die Zerstörung Jerusalems*; and his testimony is that Schumann was at that time living a lonely life, seldom leaving his abode. This state of things may possibly be attributed to Schumann's being at the time of Hiller's visit (1839) in the midst of the law suit (of which more later) which at times flung him into the depths of depression ; at other times his life was very different from that; if we may gather a fair indication from his letters. To Madame Devrient, at whose house he lived, and who had expostulated at his noise disturbing the rest of her household, he wrote : " I cannot stay here a day longer after what you have written: so I will quit, and the sooner the better . . . It was the wretched weather, and all my troubles . . . that made me rowdy."

But the mercurial temper of genius was not far away, and humour coming to his rescue, he wrote the next morning to the good lady, but in a different tone : " I permit myself to wish Madame Devrient a very good morning ; and beg her to believe me that nothing short of personal violence will induce me to give up my rooms. My lucky star brought me to her house, and I am far too grateful for all her loving care."

And a comparison of these two with a letter of about this same time to his sister-in-law, Thérèsa, throws yet another light : " I am sure you would praise my mode of life . . . Four cigars a day at the utmost, and *no beer at all* for two months. I grow so much better, I am becoming quite conceited ; so don't praise me; *leave that to me !*

It must not be imagined that at this time Schumann was able to find publishers for any unlimited amount of the pianoforte music that he cared to compose.

The *F♯ minor Sonata*, completed in 1835, was published in the next year, but the *Carnaval* and the *Etudes Symphoniques* composed in 1834-5 did not appear until 1837. From a letter to Clara Wieck: "My Sonata is not engraved yet and the publishers will have nothing to say to me. Of course I have great hopes of Haslinger." Take another letter to Heinrich Dorn: "You may believe me that if it were not that the publishers stand in awe of an editor, there would be very little seen of *my* music."

Yet Schumann was by no means lazy in facing the difficulties of publication, and in addition to the Leipzig publishers he did not hesitate to try Vienna where he found a publisher for his *piano Sonata in F♯ minor*, Opera 14, first published by Haslinger in 1836, under the unsuitable title of *"Concert sans Orchestre."* Of this work Schumann had great expectations, but they were far from being realized. The publisher insisted upon the elimination of the *Scherzo*, so as to bring the work into general accord with its new title, and it was not until after nearly twenty years that the Sonata was published complete, as his *Second Sonata in F♯ minor*.

In Liszt's view the nature of the composition was unsuited to its title of *Concerto*, which demanded "music of brilliant character, designed to a large scale, while the subject matter of the work was of an intimate nature more suited to the Salon."

At Schumann's [request Moscheles wrote an article upon the work for the *Neues Zeitschrift*, but the virtuoso adopted a guarded attitude— and though he wrote at some length, contrived to say very little.

Fantasie pour piano.

The only work definitely known to have been composed in the year 1836, is the *Fantaisie* Opus 17, published in 1839. It bore as a motto a verse from Fr. Schelgel, which may be freely rendered thus :

> There is never a chord we send on its path vibrating
> Across the chequer of dreams that we call life,
> But whispers a higher meaning to the ear,
>   Attuned to hear.

In writing to Clara Wieck when the work was published, Schumann suggested that it was she who was the higher meaning, and adds that he almost believed it. Also this :

" I have finished the *Fantasie*, and think the first movement the most impassioned I ever wrote. You can only understand it if you imagine the state of my feelings in that unhappy summer when I resigned you."

It is not easy to reconcile this with Schumann's informing his publisher (in December, 1836) that he had composed the work with the title of

Ruins, Trophies, The Starry Crown: For Beethoven's Monument; with the idea of presenting it to the Beethoven monument fund.

If this indeed was the idea, it seems to contradict his letter to Clara Wieck. If he had neither idea at the time of its composition, his linking of it with Clara seems insincere. We are left on the horns of a dilemma.

Die Davidsbündler-Tanze, Opus 6, eighteen characteristic pieces for pianoforte.

This work was composed in 1837 and, at his own expense, published the following year, the first edition bearing the names of Florestan and Eusebius as composers instead of that of Robert Schumann.

An initial, F. or E., is attached to the various numbers, which to some extent reflect the characteristics of their imaginary authors, as already exhibited by their writings in the *Neue Zeitschrift.*

No titles were appended to the different pieces, but indication for their interpretations were given, in some cases elaborated into introductory remarks, such as that for the last number : " With a twinkle in the eyes, Eusebius proclaimed the following—but quite superfluously." These dances are full of charm and imagination, piquantly contrasted, and delightfully characterized in Schumann's happiest vein. One remembers his view, often expressed, that his *Carnaval* was of little artistic value ; but his opinion of the

Davidsbündler was very different. He felt that
the work was an intellectual advance upon the
Carnaval, and from his letters to Clara Wieck
at the time of its publication we can see at least
one reason for his preference. " These dances,"
he wrote, " originated in the rarest excitement
that I can ever remember." " If ever I have been
happy while composing, it was in composing this
work. In it you will find an entire *Polterabend*"
(the German ceremony on the eve of a wedding),
" and therefore more than anything else of mine
it is completely yours."

And this brings us to the greatest influence in
Schumann's life, Clara Wieck. Schumann had
from the time of his first meeting with her, when
she was nine years old and he eighteen, an honest
admiration for her work ; but it was not until
about seven years later that we find cause to
notice any warmer feeling than that of friendship,
such as must almost inevitably have grown up
between two such sympathetic artists thrown
frequently in each other's way. In the year
1836 he seems to have declared himself with
some freedom, but doubtful success. " We will
discuss the Wiecks and Clara," he wrote (April,
1836) to his sister-in-law, Thérèse, " when we
meet. Meanwhile the position is critical . . .
either she must be entirely mine, or I can never
speak to her again."

Her father had already told Robert Schumann
that he would not be an acceptable son-in-law,

and indeed was hotly opposed to the idea of Clara's marrying anybody. " The idea of Clara with a perambulator is preposterous," said he ; and he could imagine for her nothing beyond the career of a pianist.

Early in this year (1836) he took Clara to Dresden to keep her out of Schumann's reach ; but in his absence the lovers contrived a meeting, to the fury of the father when he heard of it. In his interview with Robert, Wieck seems to have lived up to his reputation as a volcanic fighter, and ended a heated altercation by declaring that if Schumann made any further attempts to see his daughter, he would shoot him. He brought Clara home to Leipzig, insisted on her sending back all Schumann's letters, and, until the middle of the following year (1837), by forbidding Schumann his house and by keeping his daughter watched and controlled, was successful in keeping the lovers asunder.

In this trial Clara remained steadfast. Robert wavered.

In November, 1836, Schumann informed his sister-in-law, "Clara loves me as much as ever, but I am resigned to my fate. I am often with the Voigts' nowadays. Such is the whirligig of time."

Meanwhile Clara was resolute in ignoring her father's malicious tongue, though he used it freely and venomously, declining to believe any of the scandalous stories about her lover that he enjoyed retailing to her.

He went so far as to encourage his assistant, Carl Banck, who was épris with Clara, hoping he would undermine his daughter's "obstinacy." Banck undoubtedly made an opportunity to assure Schumann that Clara had forgotten him ; but as the suspicious parent shortly after took alarm at the attitude of the new suitor, he summarily dismissed him. Banck left Leipzig, and seems to have behaved badly to both the lovers, for when they came together again, they joined in fixing the blame on him as having been the means of keeping them so long asunder.

In August, 1837, Clara Wieck gave a recital in Leipzig ; Schumann, attending it, found his *F♯ minor sonata* in her programme. Clara gave a delightful explanation to her lover : " It was my only chance of showing you my inmost heart. There was no chance of doing so in private, so I just did it in public."

She also had the pluck to take the initiative by sending to Schumann his friend E. A. Becker, on the pretext of asking for the return of his letters that Wieck had sent back to him. The day after the recital the lovers became definitely plighted (14th August, 1837).

On Clara's eighteenth birthday, the following month, Schumann wrote to Wieck making a formal demand for the hand of his daughter. Becker advised him as to the letter, and in it Schumann most reasonably offered to be considered as being on probation for a further eighteen months during which he would communicate with Clara only by letter. Another stormy interview with Wieck followed, ending in a declaration of war ; and within a month Clara left Leipzig for a concert tour, accompanied by her father. During her tour the lovers resorted to every subterfuge for the exchange of letters through mutual friends ; but after Clara's return to Leipzig in the following May (1838) they contrived to see far more of each other, and by August it was agreed that, with or without the father's consent, they would be married as soon as Clara came of age (1840).

Schumann's two years preceding his betrothal had been filled not only with his distasteful struggle with Friedrich Weick, but also with periodical doubts of Clara, sufficiently distressing to render the life of so sensitive a man as Robert Schumann well nigh unbearable. There were times when he revelled in the idea of his love, and joyed in the constant necessity of their correspondence being conducted clandestinely, a plan that precisely fitted his humour of secrecy. At such times his musical nature expressed itself in glowing colours, and the *Fantasiestücke für das Piano* (Opus 12) is one of the fruits. It was composed in 1837, and published in the following year.

Each of the pieces of this series may be correctly described as a poem, and the two books of them undoubtedly contain some of the most inspired of Schumann's piano compositions.   In his view the various numbers of his *Carnaval* killed each other, but in these " one may settle down in comfort."

His favourite was *In der Nacht* (in the second book), and in writing to Clara he told her :

" No sooner had I composed it, than I was enchanted to find that my music contained in it the story of Hero and Leander.   As I played it, the incidents rose up before my eyes : Leander's plunge into the waters of the Hellespont—Hero's call—his response—he gains the shore, and then the cantilena that I have thrown round their embrace.   At last the agony of parting, and the darkness of the night that covers everything."

As with this *In der Nacht*, so with the others : they overflowed from his heart in a stream of melody.

Schumann considered some of them unsuitable for performance in public, no doubt recognizing in them the almost unique sense of personal intimacy that pervades so much of his music.

In a letter to Henriette Voigt about this work, we find : " Some music is difficult to read and strange, like many a composer's handwriting ; but once you have grasped its meaning, you wonder how any other could have suggested itself."

CHAPTER IX

1838—1840

The Neue Zeitschrift—Vienna—Difficulties—The *G minor piano Sonata*—*Kinderscenen*—*Kreisleriana*—*Novelletten*—return to Leipzig—editing the Neue Zeitschrift—Wieck's enmity—*Three piano Romances*—*Arabeske*—*Blümenstück*—*Humoreske*—*Nachtstücke*—*Faschingsschwank Aus Wien*—Liszt—The year of Song—The songs—Schumann's marriage.

THE event last recorded was the determination of Clara Wieck and Schumann to marry, either with or without the parental consent, as soon as Clara became of age. The intervening three years to which they had to look forward promised to be a period of difficulty ; but the value of this definite decision to overcome all obstacles cannot be over-estimated in its relation to the development of Schumann's character.

He had begun his musical career as an affected *dilettante*, and it was not until forced to a decision that his development began. We have seen him also a *dilettante* in his affairs of the heart ; but from the time of this decision we find his character growing in strength and in determination, and the man, in fact, beginning to develop into the lovable personality that we recognize through his music.

The financial condition of the *Neue Zeitschrift*

für Musik was fairly satisfactory ; but it appeared to Schumann likely that if the paper were published in Vienna, it would gain in prestige, and extend its influence more rapidly.

Clara was of the same opinion ; so after having arranged for Robert Friese to take over the editorship, Schumann left Leipzig for Vienna at the end of September (1838), hoping to transfer the publishing of the paper there by the beginning of the following year. The Vienna correspondent of the paper, J. Fischoff, engaged an apartment for him, and Schumann set about making the necessary arrangements. After Leipzig he found Vienna disconcertingly large, and his letters represent him as being met with unforseen difficulties and delays to such an extent, that by the end of October he wrote to his Leipzig publisher that he saw little prospect of being able to arrange the transfer before July instead of January.

Meanwhile, though received by a few aristocrats, he was not making much progress in the musical world, where Rossini opera and other music of the same type was carrying everything before it. His intimate companions were Fischoff, and Wolfgang Mozart, son of the composer ; and he wrote to Zwickau that Vienna was so full of cliques, that to get a proper footing he would need more of a " snake-like nature " than he possessed. Serious music being unfashionable, and all the musicians scrambling among the lighter kinds of music " like flies in buttermilk," he felt himself solitary in Vienna and soon grew discouraged.

He visited the graves of Schubert and Beethoven and on the latter found a steel pen, left there by a visitor. He decided to preserve it " as a sacred thing " ; but thought better of it later, and put the pen to good use, by writing with it the score of his *symphony in B♭* Opus 38.

By the middle of December he wrote to Thérèse Schumann that he would " go back to Leipzig *to-morrow* if he could," for he was still living in a state of being passed on from one official to another with a view to making the necessary arrangements. " I doubt," he wrote, " whether all the talk of the good humour of the Viennese means anything more than agreeable faces."

He made the acquaintance of Ferdinand Schubert, the composer's brother ; and at his house, found a number of unpublished works, " including masses, symphonies and operas," which the brother was taking no steps to publish. Among them was the *C major Symphony*, of which Schumann arranged a performance in Leipzig under Mendelssohn in 1840.

During the year 1838, Schumann brought to completion his own *Second Piano Sonato*, and composed the *Kinderscenen*, the *Kreisleriana*, the *Novelletten* and *Four Piano Pieces*.

Schumann had begun the composition of his

Second Piano Sonata, Opus 22 (in G Minor), five years before he completed its last movement in 1838. Clara Wieck produced the work in Berlin two years later, and recorded that it made a great success.

The *Kinderscenen* (Opus 15) consists of thirteen short pieces for piano, provided with suggestive titles. They are among the most characteristic of his early works, and Schumann said they came into being owing to Clara's remarking that in some respects he " seemed to her like a child." He described them as peaceful, tender, happy music.

This from a letter to her : " After composing some thirty little pieces, I chose a dozen of them, and put them together under this title. You will like them."

In a letter to Heinrick Dorn (September, 1839), after complaining of the stupidity of a Berlin critic who " imagines that I set before me a yelling child, and then set about finding music that sounded like its howling," he insisted that though certain children's faces were sometimes in his mind the titles " were of course added afterwards," by way of hints of the conception and interpretation.

It is not easy to reconcile this with his statement elsewhere that his *Kinderscenen* were " a grown man's reminiscences of his own childhood." From an article by Cyril Scott, entitled *Schumann*, *the master of child music*, I borrow a suggestive passage :

"He was the messenger from the heart of the child to the heart of the parent. Nay, he was more : he was the true poet of the child-soul, of the child-nature, of the child-life. With his tenderness, his whimsicality and his humour ; with his questionings, his fancifulness, his pleadings and his dreaminess ; he implanted in the mother-heart the true likeness of the child ; and she understood . . .

"His music affected the subconsciousness of the child-soul in a manner in which none hitherto have been capable. It was the only music so far conceived which was attuned to the child-mind, and for this reason it was equally the only music capable of *educating* the child."

The *Kreisleriana*, Opus 16. These eight fantasies were composed in the same year as the *Kinderscenen* and published at once in Vienna.

From a letter to an admirer :

"I like the *Kreisleriana* best of all my recent compositions (i.e. 1838). The title means nothing except to Germans, and those who know Kreisler"—E.T.A. Hoffman's creation—an erratic, wild but gifted *Cappellmeister*.

He told Dorn that this composition, and also the *Davidsbündler* and *Novelletten* were entirely inspired by his love for Clara Wieck.

From a letter to her (April, 1838)

" Since last I wrote to you, I have written a whole book of new things. I shall call them *Kreisleriana*, but it is you, and the thought of you, that play the chief part : so it is you to whom they must be dedicated, no one else. You shall recognize yourself in them and smile . . . My music of to-day is much more involved, and despite a seeming simplicity, is eloquent of the heart to everyone I play it to."

It is strange to note that when published they were none the less dedicated to Chopin.

The *Novelletten* (Opus 21) were also composed at a time when Schumann described himself as writing, more than ever, straight from the heart ; though a year later he told his friend Hirschbach that they were " on the whole light and superficial, excepting one or two places where I got deeper."

He described them in a letter to his friend, J. Fischoff (Vienna correspondent of the *Neue Zeitschrift*), as being " long, connected, adventurous stories," and in writing to Clara (February, 1838) he described the work as comprising " Jests, Egmont stories, scenes with parents, and a wedding," but no individual titles were given.

He adds : You appear in them in every possible situation . . . and I confidently assert that no one could have composed those

Novelletten without knowing your eyes, nor without having kissed your lips."

The only other compositions of the year were the *Four Pianoforte Pieces* (Opus 32) that remained unpublished until 1841. They were severally entitled *Scherzo*, *Gigue*, *Romance* and *Fughette ;* and they probably served to fill in stray hours of a busy year. Before starting for Vienna however, we learn from a letter to his correspondent there, that he had been working at a string quartet " which obsesses me at present, and makes me very happy, although it is only an experiment."

By the following March (1839) Schumann reluctantly decided to abandon the idea of establishing either his paper or himself in Vienna. The interminable difficulties with officials in obtaining a government licence to publish the *Neue Zeitschrift* there, were more than he could cope with. He was thoroughly discouraged ; and on hearing from Thérèse of the serious illness of his brother Edouard, he hurriedly left the city.

On reaching Leipzig the first news he received was that of the sudden death of his brother ; and the next was that Wieck had sent Clara to Paris chaperoned by a French lady.

It was a wretched homecoming ; and he felt that from Vienna he had brought home little save six months' experience of life in an unfriendly foreign capital.

Vienna had tired him of journalism for the moment, and he wrote to Heinrick Dorn (April, 1839) : " If only I could give up the paper altogether, and instead of getting mixed up with all the petty troubles attached to editing, devote all myself to music like a true artist ! " Yet within a month he had taken up the reins with fresh energy ; and he wrote to Hirschbach, one of his composer-contributors :

" Depend upon me, I am firmly seated in the saddle, and shall find a way through the darkness and tangle."

Schumann allowed himself a very free hand in the editing and " arranging " of his various contributors' work. From a letter to Dorn, who had composed an opera, *Schöffe von Paris :*

" I found an essay here on your opera, but put it aside as being too Finkian in tone. But I shall re-arrange it, and publish it soon." He did.

The eighteen months that followed on his return to Leipzig were fully occupied. When in Vienna he had composed " a good deal, but not in my best style," but his return to the scene of battle nerved him to renewed exertions in all directions.

A final appeal was made to Friedrich Wieck, but without success ; and acting under advice, the lovers decided to apply for a legal process to compel his compliance.

Wieck was furious with both of them, and as he

forbade Clara his house, she found a temporary home with his mother (now become Frau Bargiel) in Berlin. He circulated slanderous letters indiscriminately attacking their morals ; but in these distressing circumstances his daughter developed a self-reliance and a staunchness that he had little expected of her. As a final move, he put in a preposterous plea that Schumann was well known to be a drunkard, and by this attack the impressionable Schumann was brought to the brink of despair. From a letter to Becker (July 1839) :

" I hardly think I shall live to hear the Court's decision in our case . . . my grief is frantic."

The death of his friend Henriette Voigt in the middle of October was another blow at a time when he was in no fit state to receive it.

Throughout these eighteen months the brightest spot was undoubtedly Clara's gallant bearing in the face of adversity ; but others were not altogether wanting, and the conferring of the honorary degree of Doctor of Music by the University of Jena gave Schumann very real pleasure.

He wrote to Dorn that " the struggle that I have to carry on with Wieck about Clara, is to a certain extent reflected in my music." But it was not only the struggle that was reflected, and indeed it could not have been otherwise. " Mental and physical experiences, literature and surroundings always influence one ; and now I

ask myself where it will end " (letter to Edward
Kruger, June, 1839).

He told Hirschbach he was " living through
some of the Beethoven quartets to the fullest
extent, and realizing in himself the love and the
hate that lie in them."

At times he was able to get away from the
tragedy of it all, to concentrate upon his work,
or even to joy in some of the music of the
past.

" *The* Bach," wrote he, " is like my Bible—
day by day." And again : " The thoughtful
combinations, the poetry and humour of our
modern music, can all be traced back to Bach.
All the romantic composers approach Bach far
more nearly than Mozart ever did : all of them
know him thoroughly, and, I myself confess my
sins every day to that mighty one, and endeavour
to strengthen and refine myself through him
. . . he is unfathomable." And then we
find a reminiscence of Jean Paul Richter : " Air
and praise are the two things a man can and must
have."

In December (1839) he wrote to Becker that
excepting three romances, he had not been able
to finish anything, though he had begun countless
pieces. Nevertheless during the year he completed five other works for the piano.

From Clara's letters we learn that she
particularly admired *The Three Romances*, Opus
28, and asked to have them dedicated to her.

Schumann replied that although he was far from thinking them good enough for her, he would of course do so. But when they were published they bore a totally different dedication. These *Romances* were always among Schumann's favourite piano compositions.

All the other works of this year were published in Vienna—*Arabeske*, Opus 18; *Blumenstück*, Opus 19; *Humoreske*, Opus 20; *Nachtstücke*, Opus 23; and *Faschingsschwank Aus Wien*, Opus 26.

Of these Schumann thought the first two of little importance; but not so the *Humoreske*, although in a letter he refers to its being melancholy stuff.

During their composition, Schumann informed his fiancée : " All the week I have scarcely left my piano, composing and laughing and crying, all together. So my *Humoreske* is the result, and you will find it all there." And the work indeed does contain it all ; for it is one of Schumann's most individual works, full of the German humour that he describes as made up of wit, fancy and kindliness. It is a breezy work, compact of the short musical figures that so perfectly suited Schumann's style and methods of composition, and that not only lend themselves to variety of treatment but seem almost to ask for it. One feels the spring in this work, and knows it must have been composed in a poet's happy hour. Infinite riches in a little room.

The *Nachtstücke* are four night pieces, the
first of which Schumann composed with a second-
sighted sense of death about him. His brother,
Edouard, was in fact dying; but at the time he
composed the *Funeral Cortège*, he had not had
the news. "I could see funerals, coffins, and
miserable, desperate people: I could hear the
sigh of a breaking heart."

The *Faschingsschwank Aus Wien* is a series of
five pieces, Viennese Carnival fooleries, that
Schumann represents in his letters as "romantic
show pieces." Into one of them, the first, the
Marseillaise, officially tabooed in Vienna at that
time, was ingeniously smuggled. A spirit of
mischief suggested this, owing to all the bothers
that Viennese officialdom had put in his way;
but such a humour is scarcely conducive to the
production of a masterpiece.

We have now reached the year 1840, a notable
year in Schumann's life, to which an important
touch was added by the arrival of Liszt at Leipzig.
It was the first meeting of the two musicians,
though they had already been in correspondence,
and the effect upon the sensitive Schumann of
the virtuoso's playing was at first overwhelming.
Its variety amazed him: "Delicacy, strength,
sweetness and madness, and all in one moment."
And again: "This is no longer the man playing
upon an instrument, it is the revelation of a
daring mind."

A side light is thrown upon the musical outlook

of the day by finding in a single programme
of a Gewandhaus' Concert the Bach triple
concerto (in which Liszt, Mendelssohn, and
Hiller took part), and Liszt's fantasia upon airs
from Donizetti's opera, *Lucia di Lammermoor* !

Despite his intimacy with Liszt, and his admiration for his genius, Schumann's letters show that
fuller knowledge revealed characteristics of Liszt's
methods that were distasteful to him. From a letter
to Clara : " In your art, and in mine sometimes
when I am composing, there is a fine thought-
fulness that I would not sacrifice for all Liszt's
magnificence . . . I sometimes find too much
tinsel upon it."

But he was highly delighted with Liszt's
interpretation of some of the *Novelletten*, for
though much of it was played in a spirit not a
little surprising to the composer, it was " always
with genius."

It was this wonderful year of 1840 to which
Schumann was wont to refer as his " year of
song." With the exception of a few boyish
trifles, that he had either destroyed or suppressed,
Schumann's finished compositions up to this year
had been for the piano only : the only important
exceptions being the experimental *symphony
in G*, composed in 1832-1833, but never
published.

Knowing Schumann's ingrained love of poetry,
it is not a little strange that up to his thirtieth

year, the idea of composing songs seems not to
have occurred to him.

"The piano is becoming too limited for my
ideas," he wrote to Dorn in April, 1839; but
it was not to song he was then looking, but to
the orchestra, in writing for which "I have had
but little experience up to now."

A couple of months later, "I have always
considered songs as being on a lower level than
instrumental music, indeed I have not looked
upon song as a great art." Yet by February
in the next year (1840) : "At present I am writing
nothing but songs ; songs large and small, and
a few quartets for men's voices." And again to
Clara in the same month, "Oh, what bliss to be
writing songs ! and I have neglected it all these
years ! " In May, "I compose so fast, it is
almost unnatural : but I could sing myself to
death, like the nightingale." He was indeed
overwhelmed in song, and it was his love of Clara
that had opened the flood gates.

I do not wish here to discuss individual songs,
for indeed all are, in some way, individual,
clothed in a mantle of colour so personal to the
poem, that any other musical setting seems
unnecessary. Yet there have been other settings ;
but it is Schumann's genius that can convince
us as we hear his songs that his are the true
interpretations of the poems in music.

This miraculous year for Schumann saw the
birth of more than an hundred songs :

Opus 24   Liederkreis—poems   by   Heinrich
          Heine.
Opus 25   Myrthen, a set of songs composed as an
          offering to his bride, of which he wrote
          that they afforded a " deep look into
          the musical life of his soul." He
          selected the poems from Heinrich
          Heine, Byron, Goethe and others.
Opus 27, 36 and 40   Lieder und Gesange.
Opus 37   Twelve songs from Rückert's Liebes-
          frühling, composed jointly with Clara.
Opus 31   Three Ballads (by Chamisso).
Opus 35   Liederreihe (by Kerner).
Opus 39   Liederkreiss (Eichendorff).
Opus 42   Frauenliebe und Leben (Chamisso).
Opus 45 and 53   Romanzen und Balladen (Heine,
          Eichendorff, etc.).
Opus 48   Dichterliebe (Heine).

Up to this golden year Schumann had made no
study of the human voice ; and to this must be
attributed the fact that so great a proportion
of these beautiful songs, beautiful alike in conception and in workmanship, are so difficult to
sing, or are not *becoming* to the voice in the same
way that his piano part is invariably becoming to
the instrument.

In writing for the pianoforte, there was never
a difficulty of technique but he was able to mould
it to overcome any lack of unity between the
most subtle expression of the musical sense and

the quality of instrumental sound that had to convey it. It is unhappily impossible to claim for Schumann anything approaching an equal degree of aptness, or so accomplished a technique, in his treatment of the voice.

In the earlier songs the accompaniments were drawn on simple lines, generally being the merest background to the voice. By gradual degrees, however, the figures characteristic of his treatment of the solo piano began to appear. With this came a greater independence of his instrumental parts, and a freer handling of his countersubjects, producing more and more the impression of a duet between voice and instrument; while to his *postludes* he gave ever-increasing importance, sometimes winning from them beautiful and unexpected effects.

A study of these songs of Schumann's confirms one's impression that the secret of their charm lies in their spontaneity, and in the profundity of their poetic suggestion. One feels that he lived a romance in every song he wrote, and they have the power of inducing in others, in extraordinary measure, the condition of mind that needs the weaving of romance to the completion of its well-being.

The wide appeal of his songs in Germany may be attributed in no small extent to the way in which many of his simpler songs reflected the spirit of the German *Volkslied*; but the world-appeal has probably been far deeper in the case of

those of his songs that more profoundly suggest
the inmost spirit of the poems, that are to a greater
extent a re-utterance of the poet's thought than
mere folksong can ever be; for there was
probably never a composer who joyed more than
Schumann in identifying himself with the view-
point of a poet, in weaving into his re-utterance
of the poem the poet's beauties of diction, and his
subtleties of expression.

One is rather apt to underrate to-day the extent
of Schumann's invention in the art of song;
and, indeed, to see it in its true perspective it is
necessary to bear in mind that the ideal of song-
writing handed down from the eighteenth
century to the nineteenth was an artificial culture
deriving its entire beauty from its music, the
words being either negligible, or treated as
negligible.

True, Schubert had pointed the way, but
Schumann, in following his lead, did so by no mere
imitation, but wrote straight from the heart.

In such a spirit, then, full of happy promise,
and with music surging in his heart, did Robert
Schumann reach the height of his desire. The
circumstances of his three years betrothal had
brought him at times to the verge of despair, but
Clara's guiding hand had helped him to mount
again to the heights; so, at the little village of
Schönefeld, near Leipzig, on the 12th September,
1840, the lovers were married.

CHAPTER X

1841—1844

Songs—The *B♭ Symphony*—Sketch of *C minor Symphony*—
Overture, Scherzo and Finale for Orchestra—*D minor Symphony*
—*Fantasia for piano and orchestra*—*Paradise and the Peri* (the
poem)—Three string quartets—The *Piano quintet*—The *Piano
quartet*—*Fantasiestücke for Violin 'Cello and Piano*—Schumann's
home life—Schumann reviews his position—*Andante and
variations* for two pianos—*Paradise and the Peri*—Leipzig
Conservatorium—Russian tour—Illness—Editorship given up—
Journey to Dresden.

" I can scarcely tell you," wrote Schumann,
" how I enjoy writing for the voice after all my
work for the piano ; I sit at work in a perfect
ferment. But new ideas are coming ; I am even
dreaming of an opera ; but that is out of the
question so long as I continue to edit the
Neue Zeitschrift."

Then in a letter to Kossmaly : " In your essay
on song it vexed me to see that you put me in the
second class.

" I do not ask you to include me in the first rank,
but I think I have the right to a place of my own."

By the end of the year (1840) he says :

" I dare not promise better songs than I have
already accomplished, for what I have done in that
direction satisfies me."

Yet after the floodtide of song it was not to opera that he turned, but to symphonic music. Early in the next year (1841) he wrote to his contributor, Wenzel: "I have just finished the outline of a work, over which I have been perfectly blissful, but it has left me exhausted. It is incredible to me that I have finished it. Fancy, a whole Symphony; but the score is not yet written out."

This work was the B♭ *Symphony* (known as the First Symphony) Opus 38. Schumann's experience with the production of his early attempt (his *Symphony in G*, 1833) warned him to take the precaution of discussing his string parts with a specialist.

He accordingly approached Christoph Hilf, a leading violinist, who willingly did what was needful; and the symphony was first performed at a concert given by his wife at the Gewandhaus, Leipzig, on 31st March, 1841.

Mendelssohn conducted it; and although the first performance disclosed faults in the instrumentation, these were afterwards corrected.

His original intention was to name the work *A Spring Symphony*, giving to the movements separate titles: *The Coming of Spring, Evening, Happy playmates*, and *Full Spring ;* but abandoning the idea, he contented himself with sending to the poet, Adolph Böttger, a few bars of the symphony with a charming letter to tell him that a spring poem of his had brought the inspiration.

In January (1841) Clara recorded her joy that her husband had at last found scope for the exercise of his great imagination ; and we learn from her diary that the symphony cost him many a sleepless night.

The sketch was begun on 23rd January, and finished on 26th ; the score was completed by the end of February.

In a letter to Spohr, Schumann wrote that descriptive colouring was no part of his intention, but admitted that " the conditions under which he wrote the work might have influenced it."

Yet, writing to a conductor who was about to perform the symphony, we find : " Do inspire the orchestra with something of the Spring longing that obsessed me when I composed it. At the opening, let the trumpet-call be the summons to awaken. Then in what follows suggest the tender green of spring ; even the flutter of a butterfly. In the *allegro* show the coming together of all the elements of springtime. These are only fancies that came after the work was finished ; but I cannot help thinking of the last movement as Spring's farewell ; therefore I should not like it to be treated too lightly."

The reception of the work at its first hearing was undoubtedly cordial, Schumann writing that it was received with a degree of sympathy " such as I do not believe has been given to any symphony since Beethoven," and he did not hesitate to send an irate letter to his contributor Wenzel who had

sent a criticism of the work to *Leipziger Zeitung*:
" I am much hurt by what you wrote : such tepid
words from you after the work being received
with such enthusiasm ! And it *surprised* you ?
I hate such an expression like poison ! "

Clara wrote that the production of the
Symphony was a triumph over all cabals and
intrigues. " I never heard a symphony so much
applauded. Mendelssohn conducted it, and
happiness shone out of his eyes."

According to Schumann the Symphony was
" conceived in a fiery hour " : it was freely
discussed, and much which nowadays seems
rather ordinary was then new to the public, and
served to engender interest and increase the
composer's prestige ; one enthusiast made an
arrangement of the work for eight hands on
two pianos, that Schumann informed his publisher
was " admirably effective."

Close upon the heels of the first Symphony
followed three other orchestral works, besides
the sketch for a *Symphony in C minor*, which,
however, was never completed.

The *Overture, Scherzo and Finale*, Opus 52,
composed in April-May (1841) is chiefly remarkable for the middle movement, the romantic
scherzo in gigue-rhythm. Of this elaborate
work Schumann wrote : " It differs from a
symphony, in that its different movements can
be played separately. The overture should make
a good effect, but the whole work has a bright and

happy character, for I composed it in a merry mood."

The *Symphony in D Minor*, in its original form intended as a Symphonic Fantasia, was finished by September in time for his wife's birthday. Though more passionate in feeling than the *B♭ Symphony*, the music is otherwise similar in character. The whole work is intended to be played without pauses between the movements, and the construction is of an original kind that binds the whole together into one big design.

These two works were given their first performances at the last Gewandhaus concert of the year, but did not, according to the composer, repeat the success of the *B minor Symphony*.

" It was probably too much of me at a single sitting ; and we missed Mendelssohn's conducting too ; but it doesn't matter, for I know the things are good, and will make their way in their own good time."

Ten years later he revised the Symphony, and it became known as the Fourth (Opus 120).

The *Fantasia in A Minor for piano and orchestra* eventually became the first movement of the *pianoforte concerto*, Opus 54. The original work was, however, complete in itself, and probably remained so in the composer's mind for a period of nearly four years.

" One thing that makes me happy," he wrote in his diary, "is the knowledge of still being far from my ultimate goal : and the feeling that it is within my power; to reach it, obliges me to go on doing better work."

After completing all this orchestral music, his thoughts turned again to opera. " Reviewing my compositions," he wrote, " I find much that gives me pleasure ; but all that is nothing in comparison with my happy dreams for the future. Can you guess what is the subject of my daily prayers ? *German opera.* There I see a worthy field."

But the reading of Thomas Moore's poem, " Lalla Rookh," brought him face to face with a different type of subject, though one after his own heart, in *Paradise and the Peri,* and the idea of opera was put aside.

" It has made me utterly happy, and perhaps I can make out of it something fine for music " ; and after working at the arrangement of the " book " with his friend, Fleisig, from time to time throughout the next year, Schumann began the composition of the music in February, 1843.

Before we come to that time, we have yet to deal with the intervening year, 1842, which was devoted to Chamber music, with the interposition of a concert tour and a trip to the Bohemian Spas. On the first of these they visited Bremen and Hamburg, where in March the *B♭ Symphony* was given, though ill-fortune drew them to the latter city at the time of the four-days' fire that destroyed about a quarter of it, including most of its public buildings.

From Hamburg Clara went on alone to concerts in Copenhagen, and Schumann returned to Leipzig, to composition; where the *Three String quartets* of Opus 41 (in A minor, F major and A major) were completed before August. Moritz Hauptmann, the great critical authority of his day, expressed himself as being highly pleased with the quartets, which is as much as saying that at least in his opinion Schumann adhered to classical models. Like every other composer, Schumann thought at the time of their composition, that these, his latest works, were his best, and was greatly distressed when the celebrated Müller quartet, of Brunswick, pronounced them uninteresting, and returned them to their publisher.

These quartets underwent manifold revision before they reached the form in which we now know them, and he also experienced considerable difficulty about the publication of anything beyond the separate " parts."

Writing in 1847, to Dr. Hartel, the publisher :
" Would you publish the score of one of the quartets now, and the others later . . . Quartets published only ' in the parts ' seem to me like a man who has been quartered ; one doesn't know where to catch hold of him."

Thoroughly exhausted with the effort of completing the quartets, he took Clara on a trip to Bohemia (August, 1842) taking the waters at Marienbad, and Carlsbad, and visiting Königswart.

Refreshed by the holiday, Schumann no sooner reached home than he plunged into fresh composition, and in quick succession produced the *Quintet for strings and piano ; Quartet for strings and piano ; The Fantasiestücke for violin 'cello and piano.*

The *Piano Quintet,* Opus 44, finished in October (1842) was first played at a music party given by Herr Voigt (in December) with Mendelssohn at the piano, and as the result of a criticism of his, Schumann re-wrote the second trio. He received twenty Louis d'or from his publisher for this work, the success of which was instantaneous.

It was, indeed, pronounced the best piece of Chamber music since Beethoven, and, strange to say, this dictum of the time has not since been overset. Schumann wrote of the work as being " very spirited and full of life." It is, indeed, compact of happiness, poetry, energy and originality, and all combined with the unerring touch of genius.

Such a work is to the weary-minded a joy, and to the lover a revelation.

The *Piano Quartet in E flat* (Opus 47) is another of the masterpieces of Chamber music, full of the intimate beauty of which Schumann, in his great moments, possessed the secret. Strangely enough its first public performance was deferred until December, 1844.

The *Fantasiestücke* (Opus 88) being four

pieces for Violin, 'cello and Piano, were also laid aside after completion at the end of 1842, and were not published until 1850. Schumann wrote of the work : " It is quite unlike the quintet and quartet, and is of a very delicate nature."

Meanwhile the married life of Clara and Robert Schumann was of the happiest. They were content to live a home life of rare seclusion ; and each of them was large-minded enough to rejoice whole-heartedly in the other's artistic successes. Schumann was always at his happiest when he was composing works destined to be introduced by his wife ; and she, in turn, rejoiced in her privilege of standing between her husband and the audience as his interpreter. I do not think it can be held that he in any way diverted the natural bent of his genius in order to make it chime in with that of his wife ; it was just the happy conjunction of two artistic entities, utterly sympathetic in outlook and in method.

At such times as the exigencies of composition called for the readjustment of the hours of practice necessary to Clara as pianist, she readily made it, and happily.

" I sometimes hear D minor booming through the house," wrote Clara, " and know there is another work being created in the depths of Robert's soul."

And it was, indeed, the beginnings of his *D minor Symphony* that she referred to on that occasion.

As Clara Wieck, Madame Schumann had created for herself a position as a piano-virtuoso of the first rank, and in a period, too, when that class contained such names as Moscheles, J. B. Cramer, Chopin and Liszt; but up to the time of her marriage, she had been content to let her programme consist largely of such bravura music as that of Friedrich Pixis or Heinrich Herz, the popular Parisian-Austrian, whose music Mendelssohn refused to listen to, and whom Schumann chaffed so unmercifully in the *Zeitschrift für Musik*.

Her husband's influence upon her development as a musician (in differentiation to her development as a pianist) soon made itself felt, and by degrees she devoted herself more and more to the congenial task of popularizing his compositions that she loved so well. She expressed herself as being no ardent admirer of women composers, and, indeed, in her day they were of indifferent value; but still protesting her own lack of talent as a composer, she none the less produced some delightful music. But it was not until Schumann's year of Chamber music (1842) that she learned to appreciate the beauties of the string quartet, admitting frankly that up to that time it had bored her.

Under her husband's capable guidance she also explored the realms of poetry, particularly the works of Shakespeare, of which she knew but little, and widened her musical sensibilities.

It must not be thought that Schumann was so self-centred as to accept without qualms the sacrifices his wife had frequently perforce to make : " Sometimes it is impossible for her to get the practice needed to secure mechanical infallibility," wrote he, " and that is my fault. Of course Clara recognizes the necessity of my using my talent now when it is at its best. I suppose there must be something of this in a marriage of artists ; but the principal thing is that we are utterly happy, understanding and loving each other whole-heartedly."

The September of 1841 saw the birth of their first daughter, Marie, and May, 1843, the second, Lieschen.

Another source of satisfaction to Clara at this time was her reconciliation with her father, of which Schumann wrote to Verhulst : " I am glad of it for Clara's sake ; but he has offered to *forgive me too !* Surely the man must be devoid of feeling, or he would never make such a proposal."

Reviewing in this year his position as a composer, Schumann wrote to Kossmaly : " *Now* I think I am more independent." And again : " My best things for the piano are the six *Fantasiestücke*, the *Kreisleriana*, the four books of *Novelletten* and the *Romances*. . . . They are as yet little known, first, by reason of the inherent difficulties both of form and content, then because I am no virtuoso-pianist to play them in public; and, last, while *I* cannot write about them in my own paper, Fink *will not*. But the world moves on, and the public is beginning to show a little more interest."

The year 1843 also brought with it a change in the style of Schumann's compositions. He brought to completion two important works, the first of which was the *Andante and Variations for two pianos*, Opus 46, an instance of unusually free handling of this form, first performed by Madame Schumann and Mendelssohn in August of that year. In a letter to J. H. Verhulst at The Hague, Schumann wrote: "I have only heard these variations once, but they did not go really well; they want a good deal of studying. The work is elegiac in character, and I was, I suppose, rather melancholy when I wrote it."

This letter was dated June, and probably refers to a trial of the new work on the instruments for which it was originally composed, viz.: two pianos, a horn and two 'cellos. This was apparently an instance of Schumann's sense of instrumental colour having deceived him, for when he rearranged the work for two pianos, it was extremely successful.

But the large work of the year 1843 was his Cantata, *Paradise and the Peri*, designed for solo voices, chorus and orchestra, Opus 50. He wrote of it as being "an oratorio for happy people," and for about three months Schumann over-worked so assiduously at its composition that Clara dreaded the consequences to his health. After a final bout of what he called " strenuous labour," he finished it in June and wrote (to Verhulst) :

" It is my biggest work, and, I hope, my best. I wrote *Fine* at the end with my heart full of thanks to Heaven for keeping my energy at full strength until I completed it. . . . The story seems written to be set to music. . . . My work fills an entire programme, and if I can put it into my concert in the winter, I shall conduct it myself—and in that case you must be there at all costs."

And produced it was at his concert in December of that year and conducted by him. It made a success so sensational that it was repeated the following week.

Madame Schumann invited Mendelssohn, who was in Berlin at the time, to come for the second performance, but the letter was delayed in transit, so that he wrote: "I am really too disappointed about it. Tell your husband how heartily glad I am to hear on all hands of this splendid success. I feel it as if a piece of good fortune had happened to myself."

There had been considerable trouble at the orchestral rehearsal ; but Schumann wrote to his wife that it went excellently. Of the performance he wrote : " In conducting it I was inspired ; " but from all accounts Schumann as conductor was no better able to secure a fine performance of his own works than are most composers.

The soprano singer wrote to Clara, " If only your husband could persuade himself to scold a little, he would receive so much more attention."

The trouble was, no doubt, the same as at the present day, i.e., the composer, knowing the " parts " that he has put into the score, hears them so much more readily than anyone else that he fails to correct errors of balance, even if he happens to know *how* they should be remedied. That a composer is able to secure an authoritative reading of his own orchestral works is a popular fallacy that the failure of nineteen out of twenty does not suffice to eradicate.

Moore's poem, on which Schumann's work was based, is well known, and while written in a style borrowed from Byron, plumbs the depths of sentimentality. But it appealed to the sentimental streak in Schumann's nature : " It is so poetical, so pure," he wrote. It will be remembered that in the poem the exiled sprite seeks to gain admission to Paradise by bringing as an offering " the gift that is most dear to Heaven."

Her first offering is a drop of blood shed by a hero who sacrificed himself for the cause of freedom.

Next she brings the " farewell sigh of a vanishing soul " :

> " One kiss the maiden gives, one last
> Long kiss, which she expires in giving."

But for that sigh :

> " . . . the crystal bar
> Of Eden moves not,"

and the Peri is forced to seek again.

In a pictured landscape, not unlike a lithograph after Goodall, the Peri comes upon a bandit in softened mood :

> " He hung his head—each nobler aim
> And hope and feeling which had slept
> From boyhood's hour, that instant came
> Fresh o'er him, and he wept—he wept—"

and it is this ruffian's tear of repentance that gains for the Peri her reward :

> " Joy, joy for ever !—my task is done—
> The gates are passed, and Heaven is won."

The work consists of twenty-six musical numbers, wherein solo voices and chorus are used arbitrarily for the narration of the story. The soprano is also the Peri, and the contralto the angel at the gate, while the tenor and the bass double the various men's parts, and sing in the quartets.

There is much beautiful music in the work, but the whole seems somewhat lacking in a coherent design. Although Schumann thought very highly of Moore's poem, writing of it as " one of the sweetest flowers of English verse," he felt the necessity of more variety in the music than that for which he could find warrant in the text. He accordingly added many verses of his own, especially in the latter part ; but in spite of that the work remains somewhat monotonous in performance.

The suggestion of Oriental colour, in ways that have since become somewhat banal, was fresh at the time, and no doubt helped its success ; while Schumann's abandoning of the *recitativo secco* was a factor in the popularity of the work which, although of a novel form for the concert room, was not too involved to be grasped at a first hearing.

This success so greatly added to Schumann's growing prestige, that the work was produced at Dresden within a month of the Leipzig performances, and it was not long before he entered into negotiation for producing his work in London in the following year. The project fell through, owing to the difficulty of finding a publisher for the English version ; but although the libretto has since been translated into French, and retranslated into English, its popularity in this country, despite the beauty of its individual numbers, has never been so great as in Germany, where a wave of sentimentality prepared the way for its reception.

After Schumann's success with *Paradise and the Peri*, he returned to the consideration of an idea of Clara's that he should find a post as Conductor, that would be more lucrative than composition. They had discussed such a possibility before their marriage, but he had then written : " do not be too ambitious for me, I ask nothing more than you and a piano." Now, however, with the increased responsibility of two children, some such step became necessary.

Since April, 1843, Schumann had been on the staff of the Leipzig Conservatorium, an institution that, after years of effort, Mendelssohn had at length succeeded in founding under the patronage of the King, with himself as Director, teacher of singing, composition and piano.

Schumann was also to teach the piano, composition and score-reading, but as there were only forty students in all, it is not to be imagined that Schumann's fees amounted to any considerable sum, and he felt bound to make some special effort to increase his income. Consequently, at the beginning of the following year (1844) the Schumanns set out upon a concert tour in Russia. Madame Schumann gave concerts in Mitau, Riga, three in Moscow, where they stayed four weeks, and four in St. Petersburg.

The first two of these were not well attended, Schumann writing that everyone in St. Petersburg was mad about Italian opera.

News of Clara's brilliant playing spread rapidly and her third and fourth concerts were immensely successful. She was commanded to play at Court, and Count Wielhorsky gave a princely soirée, in honour of the Schumanns, engaging a full orchestra to play Schumann's B♭ *Symphony*, which the composer conducted.

Another function in St. Petersburg was Prince Peter of Oldenburg's, when Henselt and Madame Schumann played her husband's variations for two pianos.

Schumann had been warned to expect terrible difficulties when travelling in Russia ; but he wrote that " it is neither better nor worse than elsewhere, unless, indeed, it is rather better. So I can now laugh at the frightful pictures that were drawn for us at Leipzig." The thing that did amaze him was the extravagant prices of everything in St. Petersburg compared with frugal Leipzig. " Our lodging," he wrote, " costs a Louis d'or a day, coffee costs a thaler, and dinner a ducat."

Unfortunately Schumann was far from well during the whole tour, which lasted some four months ; and soon after his return to Leipzig, he decided to hand over the Editorship of the *Neue Zeitschrift* to his friend Lorenz. Writing in June (to Verhulst) : " I scarcely think I shall ever take it up again, as I want to devote myself entirely to composition."

Soon after the resumption of his work at the Conservatorium, however, Schumann's health completely broke down, and he had to hurry away to the Harz in search of a cure. Little, if any, better, he proposed to visit Dresden, and went there so ill that it almost seemed he would die before accomplishing the journey. Poor Clara was at her wit's end. "Robert could not sleep at all," she wrote; "his disordered imagination conjuring up the most terrifying pictures, to which he surrendered himself utterly, so that by morning I usually found him beside himself with weeping."

It was a case of complete nervous exhaustion; but the change to Dresden brought such satisfactory improvement, that the Schumanns decided at once upon giving up their Leipzig home with his not very congenial post at the Conservatorium, and to make their home in the capital city.

"The doctors advised the move," wrote Schumann, "and since Mendelssohn left Leipzig we no longer cared much to remain there."

There was a farewell matinée in Leipzig, and by the middle of December (1844) the Schumanns removed to Dresden.

CHAPTER XI

ROBERT SCHUMANN'S LITERARY SIDE

" Music which excites the nightingale to a love-song, sets the lap-dog barking," wrote Schumann ; and without endeavouring to show all the other contemporary writers upon music as lap-dogs, his own method of writing went far to prove him a nightingale.

The literary instinct was deep seated in Robert Schumann's nature, and patiently fostered by his father up to the time of his death in 1826. His knowledge of literature was extensive, and his enthusiasm was that of a poet : the fantasy and word painting that went to the making of his literary style, were those of a poet, and it was not until the last few years of his life that he exchanged its rhapsodical manner for the meditative calm, and something of the judicial penetration that were more generally brought to bear upon the consideration of the other arts. And yet the opinions he expressed in his most fantastic and flamboyant critiques, no less than in others that he put forward in more tentative fashion, were none the less based upon a keen insight, and in large measure are still tenable to-day.

Though many composers have since written on musical subjects, there was scarcely one who did so before Schumann, excepting Carl Maria Weber ; and the proportion of Weber's writings to his compositions was far smaller than in Schumann's case. Schumann was a rapid worker alike in music and in literature, otherwise it would have been impossible for him to produce so much music during the ten years that he was both editor of *Neue Zeitschrift für Musik* and at the same time its most voluminous contributor.

Not only did his mind work with the rapidity of genius, but he inherited from his father the invaluable gift of concentration that enabled him to work at either of his arts in the midst of peculiarly distracting surroundings.

Before launching the *Neue Zeitschrift* at the age of twenty-three, he had already contributed articles on musical subjects to various papers, and it is obvious that literature was as much a part of his artistic nature, and as much his natural medium of expression as was music.

The two arts were intermingled in his mind to an extent of which he was scarcely conscious ; but they acted and reacted, the one upon the other, in a hundred ways that are revealed in his works. One of the contradictions with which we are faced, is his frequent reiteration of his view that his music was inspired by no idea outside itself, and that the titles that he gave to his various works were added afterwards with a view to inducing in his audience a sympathetic frame of mind.

Such assertions are again and again contradicted, and indeed disproved by our knowledge of the state of his mind and of the circumstances surrounding him at the time of the composition of so many of his works ; and the fact remains that there was probably never a composer, and certainly none before his time, who in his music was influenced by literature and by ideas derived from literature, to a greater extent than was Schumann.

His idea of the function of musical criticism was to act as a sympathetic interpreter of a composer's work ; and placing himself at the composer's point of view, thus help others to a sympathy with the work not otherwise to be gained. That he experienced no difficulty in so doing is shown by his writings in the *Neue Zeitschrift*, many of which he gathered together long after he relinquished his editorship, and published under the title of *Gesammelte Schriften über Musik und Musiker* (in 1854.)

We have already seen some of the fanciful methods that he pressed into this service, such as the invention of the various characters comprised in the David-brotherhood—not only for the slaying of the musical Philistines, but for the discussion and encouragement' of music that they deemed worthy.

On one occasion, when he wished to deal in his paper with a batch of dance music, his article related in sprightly fashion the incidents of an imaginary fancy-dress ball, where the dances to be criticised constituted the entire programme. In this bolus, compounded of fanciful, sentimental and humorous happenings, and the talk of the ballroom, he contrived to convey his appreciation or criticism of the music.

One of his difficulties as editor of a musical paper was his natural diffidence in admitting to it articles dealing with his own compositions. From a letter to his Jena correspondent, Keferstein, " Your essay is a fresh mark of your good will. Parts of it, especially those that concern me, are, I am afraid, rather too enthusiastic—you will not misunderstand me ? If the essay were printed bearing your real name—though I know in your position that would be impossible—then there would be no trouble. But I imagine readers to be always inclined to suspicion of enthusiastic praise when it is anonymous. . . . The public will only believe in an article that bears the writer's signature."

Yet seeing that he was working towards the elevation of the popular taste, which he realized as being degraded by the shallow music that reigned supreme in the social world as he found it, it would obviously have been to the interest of the cause he had at heart, that a thorough explanation of what he was aiming at in music should be systematically and openly laid before his readers.

To facilitate the realization of the extent to which music throughout the period of Schumann's activity as a writer, and the major part of the period of his activity as a composer, was dominated by the school of Italian opera of the period—butterfly dust, he called it—I have made a table (at page 258) giving on the one side the date of the production of some important contemporary works, and of many others that were deemed of importance in their day : while on the other side of the table, according to the years of their composition, I have set the names of Schumann's principal works. Consideration of this table suggests something of what was going on in musical minds of his day other than his own.

Open as he was to new ideas, Schumann did not hesitate to attack where he thought it necessary. The works of Heinrich Herz were one of his butts ; and then there was again, his famous attack upon Meyerbeer's opera *Les Huguenots*—probably the bitterest article he ever wrote—in which he laid bare the tawdry theatricality that many other people have since found in the work. But his general attitude was one of *avoiding* what seemed to him to be bad or shallow music, preferring to place his pen at the service of the music that appealed to him as worthy of being praised and elucidated. He was confident that by those means he could best help forward what he liked to call the poetic phase

170

of music, as opposed to the merely formal ; and in that he undoubtedly succeeded. For his writings, while revealing his poetic talent, and bearing the impress of a breezy independence and of a lovable individuality, remain to-day among the most important contributions to the literature of music.

What Schumann chiefly needed on his arrival
at Dresden (December, 1844) was a spell of the
complete rest that is so incompatible with the
temperament of a creative artist. He was
advised that he must in any case avoid hearing
music, as its effect upon his nervous system was
too intense not to be injurious. " It went
through my nerves like a knife," wrote he ; but
it was not long before he was well enough to
miss it : " There is little music to be heard here
in Dresden, and that just suits my condition, for
music exhausts me immediately."

The Schumanns accordingly began their life
in Dresden with a period of almost complete
seclusion ; and none too soon, for Robert, whose
illness had so changed him that a friend, who
followed him to Dresden and tracked him to
his burrow, thought him still little removed from
death.

The transference of a home to the capital city scarcely has the appearance of a search for rest, but Dresden had been a quiet city since 1813, when the last Napoleonic victory in a pitched battle on the grand scale left its buildings shattered by a hundred guns.

The Dresden of Schumann's day, though not beautiful, was a pleasant place, divided into two parts (the old and the new town) by the river Elbe. The old town dates from the early thirteenth century, and towards its end was chosen by Henry the Illustrious for his capital. It is chiefly known to the world by the value of its art collections; but in Schumann's day, though lagging behind Leipzig, it was far from being negligible in regard to its music. When he made his home there, in December 1844, Schumann found two other musical celebrities already in residence.

One was Ferdinand Hiller, who had been the conductor of an established series of orchestral concerts there for some five years; and the other was Richard Wagner (then thirty-one years of age) who had already filled the similar post of music-director at Magdeburg, Königsberg and Riga, and had also suffered his three years in Paris. Since the previous year he had been Capellmeister at the Court Theatre, where he had produced his *Rienzi* and *Der Fliegende Holländer*.

With Ferdinand Hiller Schumann soon felt

himself to be on common ground, and a firm friendship sprang up between the two musicians. In Richard Wagner, however, he found a bristling personality in many respects diametrically opposed to his own. It was not a question of personal enmity; but even Wagner, the overwhelming talker, could conduct only an ill-balanced discussion with a man who, like Schumann, either would not or could not express himself. So soon, however, as Schumann was sufficiently recovered to resume the amenities of quiet social life, the two met regularly at the weekly gatherings of artists of all kinds at Hiller's; and Schumann also formed a habit of attending the Court Theatre for the study of opera, the idea of which was constantly present in his mind.

In his first year at Dresden, Schumann made a study of Byron's poem, *The Corsair*, as the possible basis for an opera, and composed an aria and a chorus for it. The project, however, was dropped, like many others; for Schumann's memoranda of this period contain notes of some twenty different subjects, ranging over many different periods, and including the *Invasion of Spain by the Moors*, a sketch for which was made for him by Von Zuccalmaglio, and another work by Thomas Moore, *Mokanna*, which, however, he laid aside considering it too soon to repeat the oriental colour of *Paradise and the Peri*.

Richard Wagner completed his opera, *Tannhäuser* during 1844, and soon after making Schumann's acquaintance in the following year, presented him with a lithographed copy of the score with a friendly greeting. In the perusal of this work Schumann found much in the handling of the orchestra to disturb him, for though himself a reformer in his own way, he was accustomed to attack with a sweep less bold than Wagner's. The realization of orchestral values was never one of Schumann's strong points in composition; and independent of the dramatic aptness of Wagner's music, he seems to have been able to gather from the score but a mediocre idea of its value as music. In a letter to Mendelssohn written just before he had heard a performance of the opera : " What does the world know, and what do the musicians know, about pure harmony ? There is Wagner with his new opera, *Tannhäuser*, a clever man, no doubt, but packed with crazy ideas, and as bold as brass. Our aristocracy raves about *Rienzi*, but I can't find in his work four consecutive bars of melody, nor even of correct writing. What can be the permanent value of this sort of thing ? I have the score before me, beautifully printed with all its consecutive fifths and octaves which no doubt he would now like to correct. But too late ! The music is not a jot better than his *Rienzi*, indeed rather weaker and less natural."

But after hearing the work given, within a few days of this letter, Schumann did not hesitate to admit his mistake, and wrote to Mendelssohn: " I withdraw much that I wrote to you after reading the *Tannhäuser* score, for in performance it comes out quite unlike my picture of it, and much of it moved me deeply."

His wife noted in the diary that the Schumanns kept together: " Robert was deeply interested, and says it is a great advance on *Rienzi*, both musically and instrumentally; but for me such music is not music at all."

Schumann also wrote to Heinrich Dorn: " I wish you could hear *Tannhäuser*: it has much in it that is deep and original, though it has its trivial moments too. I think Wagner may become of immense value to our stage, and he has the courage for it."

Within a month of the first production of *Tannhäuser*, the indefatigable Wagner, at one of the weekly gatherings of artists, produced the text of a new work, *Lohengrin*, and read it aloud. " Most of us, *especially the painters*, admired it immensely."

Few of those joining in the hue and cry of the day against Richard Wagner had the pluck to recant their hasty condemnation as promptly as Schumann; but frank though he was, and glad to admit his injustice, Richard Wagner's music never aroused in him the genial glow of enthusiasm with which he so frequently expressed his admiration for Mendelssohn, Gade, and others who saw the world through his own spectacles. Take such a passage as the following, from a letter to Mendelssohn after hearing his violin concerto : " I have no criticism of such a composition ; and simply surrendered myself to the enjoyment of it. It conjured up an image in my mind, that impressed itself there; let me tell you about it. It was a figure of one of the Graces, who, for the moment abandoning her classic calm, allowed herself the luxury of a more passionate emotion, which transfigured her into the image of the Muse herself. I wish I could paint her for you."

The last piece of work that Schumann completed before the nervous breakdown that overtook him in August (1844) was the music for a scene from Goethe's *Faust*, at the end of Part II, being the salvation of Faust. The subject was one that had been in his mind since the Spring, when he and Clara were in Russia, for in his diary he records his reading the work while lying ill at Dorpat. It is by no means certain that at the time of its composition, Schumann contemplated the subsequent addition of any further scenes.

His music was not composed with any idea of stage representation ; but was rather conceived as an oratorio for concert performance. His completion of its final chorus in August was immediately followed by his collapse, and the next we hear of the composition is in a letter to Mendelssohn, dated 24th September, 1845: "My scene from *Faust* reposes in my desk, and I dread to take it out. The sublimity of the poetry moved me to make the attempt to set it, but I doubt whether it will ever be published. If my courage comes back to me I shall set more of it."

It was nevertheless nearly three years before the first private performance of this part of the music was arranged, and we shall therefore hear nothing more of the work and of its various additions until dealing with the year 1848.

The most important work completed in Schumann's first year in Dresden (1845) was the *Pianoforte Concerto in A minor*, of which the first movement, the *Fantasia*, composed in 1841, although tried by the Gewandhaus orchestra, had been laid aside. The finished work consisted of three movements, *Allegro affettuoso*, *Intermezzo* and *Allegro vivace*, the second and third movements being intended to be played without a break. Its first performance was at Leipzig Gewandhaus in January, 1846, and the work quickly became famous. "I am as happy as a King," wrote Clara, "at the mere thought of playing it with the orchestra." As a virtuoso Clara had always wanted from her husband something more in the direction of bravura music, and in the concerto she had it ; not that, in it, Schumann conceded any portion of his ideal for the sake of popularity. On the contrary, it is one of his most complete artistic successes. It is a spontaneous expression of the joy of living, full of exquisite moments, with many an inspired instance of sheer beauty of sound obtained by the simplest means. Not only does the first movement contain original and captivating material, beautifully handled, with the solo instrument shown to perfection in a series of romantic episodes characteristic of the composer, but it serves to introduce the succeeding movements to their utmost advantage. It is packed with genial happiness in a degree that few composers have been capable of achieving. One of his heart's desires was to make music happier ; and it must have been something of a tragedy to him to realize how often his compositions expressed the gloomier moods for which however he apologized in many a letter.

" Melancholy bats still flutter about me, though less frequently," he wrote to Verhulst, " and only music can drive them away " : yes, but they not infrequently forced themselves into the web of the music, and from there there was no dislodging them.

In this year (1845) Schumann made another thorough study of the works of Johann Sebastian Bach, and consulted Mendelssohn as to his ideas of undertaking a new edition of the *Wohltemperirte*

179

Klavier. The idea came to nothing, but his Bach studies led him to the production of a goodly batch of contrapuntal works.

Of these we have the

Sketches for Pedal-piano, Opus 58 :

A set of Six Fugues on B-A-C-H, Opus 60, composed for the same instrument, but alternatively playable on the organ :

Six pieces in canonic form for pedal-piano, Opus 56, playable alternatively by three or four hands : and

Seven piano pieces in fughetto form, Opus 126.

Four fugues for piano, Opus 72.

Schumann found the greatest pleasure in all this counterpoint : " I have not filed away so much at any other of my compositions as at these," he writes of his fugues on the name of Bach ; and at another time he went as far as to say he expected them to outlive all his other works. Although in many of these compositions Bach is undoubtedly the outstanding influence, Schumann was no pedant, and did not hesitate to give himself just as much latitude as he required, such as adding accompaniments that form no part in the strict plan of a fugue.

He offered two of these fugues to a publisher at Offenbach for the sum of ten Louis d'or, pointing out that he " need not expect them to be merely dry and formal. They are characteristic pieces, at any rate I think them so, and only their form is severe." Nevertheless they returned them with thanks.

When we remember that Schumann was still a sick man, his energy and industry seem uncanny. By September he reported himself as being " better " ; but even then he was not free of his " mysterious trouble " consisting of " a hundred places itching and twitching " ; and still in October, anything that broke in upon the simple routine of his life made him morbid and irritable. In November Hiller offered to let him share with him the conducting of some concerts he had organized, but : " I had to give it up, the strain was too great."

None the less, in the following December (1845) the sick man sketched in his *Symphony in C major*, Opus 61, and completed the scoring of the work in the course of the next year, when it was produced at Leipzig in November. Schumann at the time of its composition was still in a state of physical suffering, and when he heard the symphony performed he protested he could find illness in every bar. " It was not until I was well into the last movement that I began to feel at all well ; and anyhow the work reminds me of a desperate time, when music was the struggle between my spiritual powers of resistance and my physical suffering. "

In such circumstances it would be futile to expect to find in this symphony the buoyancy of the *B♭ symphony*, but in its stead there is greater depth, and a more profound intensity of expression within its classical form.

Musical life in Dresden, despite the presence of such men as Richard Wagner and Robert Schumann, continued to run in its accustomed rut, of which Schumann wrote to Mendelssohn, " *One* Beethoven symphony a year, *and that with ornamentation by the band ad libitum !* " But he looked forward to a speedy reformation by means of the new orchestral society formed by Hiller : " Unfortunately our audience consists almost solely of the aristocracy, and I fear we offer them music that is too good for them."

In the summer of 1846 Niels Gade came to Dresden on a visit to the Schumanns, and was a source of constant pleasure to his host and hostess, for they admired his frank nature and agreed with his views on music. Schumann held a very high opinion of the value of Gade's music. From a letter to Brendel : " My choral society is studying Gade's *Comala* ; and it seems to me that our Leipzig critics underrate this work. I feel it to be the most important composition of modern times, and the only one deserving of a laurel wreath."

The following month found Schumann again complaining of feeling too fatigued to write ; he removed with his family into a new house (in the Reitbahnstrasse) where they led a life even more secluded than before, and where Schumann seemed anxious only to withdraw himself from all contact with the outer world.

In the winter (1846-7) concert expeditions to Prague and Vienna, while introducing a distraction, scarcely seemed a prudent way of resting a sick man. Prague gave them a great reception; but in Vienna, though Clara played Schumann's *piano concerto* with success, his *Bb Symphony* was coldly received. Another trip for a Berlin concert, where he conducted a poor performance of *Paradise and the Peri*, was little, if any, more satisfactory. In a letter to Brendel in Leipzig, Schumann complained that the work was ill-prepared, and he would gladly have escaped the conducting of it. The chief cause of the trouble lay with the soprano and the tenor singers, operatic artists, who threw up their parts two days before the performance—" meanly enough " wrote Schumann, and their important parts—one of them being that of the Peri—had to be sung by amateurs : " They rarely sang the notes, to say nothing of other matters."

In February (1847) Schumann became ill again; but after his return to Dresden in the spring he undertook the formation of a new Choral Union of about seventy members. This gave him practice in conducting, in which he took the greatest interest. Under his direction the Society gave his *Paradise and the Peri*, the first of his *Scenes from Faust,* his *Requiem for Mignon* (composed in 1848), Hiller's *Geist über dem Wasser,* Gade's *Comala,* and Mendelssohn's *Athalie* and *Lobgesang.*

On Hiller's departure to take up a post at Düsseldorf, Schumann also became conductor of the *Liedertafel,* a male voice choir that Hiller had controlled for several years.

His completed compositions in this year were :

The *Pianoforte Trio in D minor,* Opus 63,— " a good deal of which," wrote he to Hiller, " I like exceedingly " ;

The *Pianoforte Trio in F major,* Opus 80 ;

Three Songs of War and Liberty, for male chorus, Opus 62 ; composed for his *Liedertafel;*

Seven Songs in Canon-form, Opus 65. These choral songs were not very successful, the part writing being ineffective and the style of the music not very appropriate to the medium. There were also *Twelve piano pieces for four hands, for Children small and large,* Opus 85.

In the summer came the musical festival at Zwickau, Schumann's native town, where he and Clara were naturally much fêted, and where the *piano concerto* and the *C major symphony* were repeated amid general enthusiasm.

It was in this year that an exceedingly regrettable misunderstanding occurred between Schumann and Mendelssohn. It was the fault of neither, but was brought about by the partisan feeling of their respective admirers. It is

sometimes considered to have been the natural outcome of the introduction of the more picturesque
and acute methods in musical journalism for
which Schumann was responsible. Up to the
time of his resignation of the editorship of the
Neue Zeitschrift, he steered it clear of partisan-
ship, and in that way contrived to interest
supporters drawn from every camp and from every
variety of the musical people that go to make up
the musical public. After his retirement in
1843 from the paper, the wide principles that he
had adopted were gradually changed, and the
editorial standpoint narrowed. The German
musical world of that day, guided by a press that
was far from regarding Richard Wagner's
challenge as a serious menace to the supremacy of
the musical gods of the moment, singled out two
composers as towering above their contemporaries;
and these two men were Schumann and
Mendelssohn. The two were freely compared
and contrasted ; and, as will happen among
enthusiasts, the devotees of the one thought
they were helping their idol by decrying the other.
In this way came into existence two cliques,
the Mendelssohnians proclaiming in him the
champion of form, while the Schumannites
maintained that nothing but the inner meaning
of music was worthy of consideration, and
placed their idol above all competition.

Now that the lapse of time has given us the
advantage of seeing the two composers in a less

perverted perspective it is obvious how little such exaggerated contentions could logically have been supported. Mendelssohn had always kept free from writing about music, but Schumann's known connection with the *Neue Zeitschrift*, which was naturally drawn into the battle, encouraged the suspicion of his being personally involved in its views. Both musicians were well known in Leipzig, where they had lived for several years, to the lasting benefit of its musical life, and it was in Leipzig that the first open attack was delivered upon Mendelssohn's music, and there too that the controversy raged with the greatest rancour. That Mendelssohn believed Schumann involved is clear from a letter written at the beginning of 1847 to Carl Klingemann, his collaborator in so many songs: " I am unable to give you an introduction to Frau Schumann, as her husband has behaved in a very questionable way to me ; and has started a very discreditable story about me here in Leipzig which, though I will not waste words over it, has most damnably extinguished my former ardour on his behalf."

There is every reason for the belief that Schumann had nothing whatever to do with the affair ; indeed, in view of his high opinion of Mendelssohn's music, and his personal affection for him, such a thing is simply incredible. It unfortunately sufficed to break off the friendship between the two men, and any chance of the matter being ultimately cleared up was rendered impossible by Mendelssohn's death, which occurred towards the end of 1847 (4th November). This was another great blow to Schumann, but his appreciation of his friend was never eclipsed. A year later in a letter to Verhulst : " When you come here you will meet us all just as before, saving alone him who was the best of all. It is just a year since he died."

And now we come to the beginning of Schumann's opera, which, after abandoning a score of other subjects, he decided in this year to compose under the title of *Genoveva*—his Opus 80.

As early as 1842, Schumann, writing in the *Neue Zeitschrift*, had endeavoured to arouse composers to the task of carrying on Weber's work in the cause of German opera, instead of leaving the field to the Italians and French ; and five years later ill luck led him to the legend of St. Geneviève. The chief traits of Geneviève, the peasant girl of Nanterre, were the undramatic virtues of holiness and purity, though they sufficed to lead to her being treated with extraordinary veneration by the rough fifth century population of Gaul. When the Francs, led by Childeric, beset the city of Paris, Geneviève and her religious sisterhood undertook the relief of the starving inhabitants, and after the fall of the city, successfully interceded with its captors, thus saving many from what was then the customary fate of the vanquished. At a later date Geneviève made Paris her home, and a few years after, when tidings arrived that the Huns, under Attila, were approaching the city, she led her nuns and consecrated virgins into one of the churches, exhorting them to join with her in averting the pending attack by the means of their prayer and by fasting. Attila fortunately changed his route, thus leaving Paris unharmed, and this happy event, naturally attributed to the influence of Geneviève, served to raise her prestige to the skies. Well satisfied with the course of events, which largely extended her influence, she continued to practise acts of charity, and piety, and died in the odour of sanctity at the ripe age of eighty-nine, eventually becoming the patron saint of Paris.

Such is the legend that appealed to Schumann as likely to provide him with the dramatic opportunities he sought ; but it is difficult to see what he found in it likely, one need not say, to grip an audience, but even to hold them decently interested. Two tragedies on the subject were already known to him, one by Ludwig Tieck (the translator of Shakespeare's plays, and of Cervantes' *Don Quixote*) and the other by Friedrich Hebbel. There was a poet of considerable local repute, Robert Reinick, living in Dresden, and as Schumann had made his acquaintance through Ferdinand Hiller, he invited him to construct an opera libretto from the material of the two tragedies. Progress dragged on slowly.

In a letter of July (1847) to Hiller, Schumann wrote : " He is a good kind fellow, this Reinick of ours, but ho ! how dreadfully sentimental ! " In short, Reinick could not make a libretto that Schumann could set ; and when Friedrich Hebbel came to Dresden, he did not hesitate to condemn whole-heartedly what he regarded as a mutilation of his own play. But as he resolutely declined to lend a hand to improve it, Schumann reluctantly abandoned the Reinick attempt altogether, and set himself to make an entirely fresh version.

CHAPTER XIII

1848—1850

DRESDEN.

Genoveva—First scenes from *Faust* produced—Political unrest—
Additions to the *Faust* scenes—"Most fruitful year"—
Manfred—*Album für die Jugend*—*Bilder aus Osten*—Small
instrumental works—*Requiem for Mignon*—*Advent hymn*—The
Dresden rising—*Lieder für die Jugend*—*Spanisches Liederspiel*—
Spanische Liebes-Lieder—*Concertstück* for four horns—The
Motet—*New Year's Hymn*—*Introduction and Allegro for piano
and orchestra*—The return to Dresden—Plans for Düsseldorf—
Genoveva produced—Concert tours—The Schumanns quit
Dresden.

IN the last months of 1847 Schumann completed
his reconstruction of the libretto for *Genoveva* ;
and in it he permitted himself to borrow freely
from both the authors Tieck and Hebbel, transferring long passages from their works to his own,
though the literary style of each of these poets
was as distinct from the other, as was either of
them from that of Schumann. By the time
this *mélange* was finished, Schumann, doubtless
feeling the legend to be more epic than dramatic,
had gradually eliminated all that had tended
to make the original story in any way touching.
This he did intentionally, in order to bring it
into accord with his theoretical conception of
opera, devised to throw into greater prominence his musical expression of the emotions.

But the ultimate result was that his work scarcely dealt at all with the more significant parts of the undramatic legend.

The composition of the music began in January (1848) and it was finished in August. In planning his musical scheme Schumann set before him as his model, or rather as his ideal, Weber's opera *Euryanthe*. Weber's work had been but a qualified success, but that was only another spur to Schumann. Few artists are aware of their limitations, and Robert Schumann probably less than most ; and his longing to see the advancement of German opera, led him to imagine the existence within himself of a dramatic instinct. With his reverence for *Euryanthe*, he set himself to compose a work that followed it in the elimination of spoken dialogue. But Schumann set himself to do it in a different way. Unfortunately he made apparently no attempt to differentiate the music of the different characters in the way which must have come without conscious effort, to a composer with any marked dramatic bent. Instead, to all his characters he gave music of the same kind, and of a kind, too, which gave no sign of its having sprung from the dramatic situation of the moment or indeed from *any* dramatic situation. His dislike of the Italian school of opera—" canary-bird music," he dubbed it—impelled him to shun the old-fashioned *recitativo*, and he substituted for it melody, generally accompanied by the full orchestra. That of course resulted in melody, introduced by melody, followed by melody and relieved by melody, and the whole thus spelt monotony.

In the autumn he wrote to Verhulst : " I finished my *Genoveva* in August, and, as the end came in sight, felt a happy conviction that much of it had been successful. And now I want to see it and hear it, but in view of the stormy aspect of the political world I have taken no step about it yet."

The storm became worse before it grew better, and we can defer any further mention of *Genoveva* for two years (until 1850).

Meanwhile, in June of 1848, a private performance of the *Scenes from Faust* was given by Schumann's society of mixed voices. The scenes given were the seven numbers that ultimately went to constitute Part III of the complete work, three numbers having been added in 1847 and another in 1848 to those composed in 1844. To his friend Nottebohm in Vienna, Schumann wrote early in July : " Outwardly things are quieter here ; but even Dresden, normally so indolent in matters political, cannot resist the pull of the universal whirlpool. But do leave Vienna, unhealthy for any musician who does not happen to be also a charlatan or a millionaire. If only the revolution would stick a bayonet in their unmusical gizzards ! . . . A week ago we did my *Faust* scenes. I think they made a deeper impression than *Paradise and the Peri*, but probably because of the magnificent verse." And this from a letter to F. Brendel : " I had the greatest pleasure from the many people who told me that my music had made them understand much of the poetry for the first time."

News of Schumann's work came to the ears of the promoters of the Goethe centenary cele- brations at Dresden, and on that occasion, 29th August, the *Faust Verklärung* received the distinction of three simultaneous public per- formances, in Dresden, Weimar, and Leipzig. At Leipzig his work was placed at the beginning of the programme, and made, probably on that account, less impression than at the other two festivals. From a letter to F. Brendel : " It was a mistake to begin the programme with a work that all through it has the character of a *conclusion*. The parts are not developed, but must follow each other quickly and smoothly up to the climax just before the final chorus."

But Schumann was greatly gratified at the success of the work in Dresden and Weimar, and in the course of the next two years made con- siderable additions to it, adding Part I and Part II, but with no definite idea of the several parts being performed as a whole. Finally in 1853 he added the overture.

The three parts are, as he described them, nothing more than unconnected scenes, chosen at different times, with no defined intention either of their constituting a single work, or, indeed, of the scenes being chosen as summarizing the whole of Goethe's work.

In the final form Schumann's *Scenes from Faust* consist of :

The overture—composed in 1853.

Part I. (*a*) A portion of the first Garden Scene between Faust and Gretchen :

(*b*) Gretchen at the shrine of the Mater Dolorosa :

(*c*) The Cathedral Scene.

The whole of Part I was composed in 1849.

Part II. (*a*) The song of the spirits at the dawn ; the sunrise ; and Faust's soliloquy : (all from Act I) : (composed in 1849).

(*b*) The scene with the four aged women (from Act V) : (composed in 1850) :

(*c*) The death of Faust (from Act V) : (composed in 1850).

Part III. The apotheosis of Faust (from the end of Act V) consisting of seven numbers, the first three of which, and the *Chorus Mysticus*, were composed in 1844 and the others in 1847-1848.

Schumann frequently wrote of the year 1848 as his most fruitful year : and there was certainly none in which he was more industrious. Immediately following his work upon the *Faust* scenes in July, he turned to Byron's dramatic poem, *Manfred*.

In this poem Schumann discovered some occult relation to *Genoveva*, and, full of enthusiasm, made rapid progress with his preliminary task of re-casting Byron's poem according to his own ideas of making it suitable for stage performances, borrowing from two translations, one of which was by Karl Böttger of Dresden.

On the 14th November Clara Schumann made this entry in the family diary : "To-day Robert brought home a bottle of champagne in which we celebrated the birth of the first part of *Manfred* completed to-day."

Schumann continued to work upon the *Manfred* music, Opus 115, which when completed consisted of sixteen numbers, the overture, melodrame, some choruses and solo work, and one entracte.

Byron made it unmistakably clear that he had not designed his " dramatic poem " for presentation on the stage, and Schumann found much to alter before he wrote his melodrame. The overture, one of his most inspired orchestral compositions, was composed first, and possibly before he had any idea of adding music for the entire poem. It is an extremely *innig* work, and was composed at the time when Schumann's development had reached its zenith ; but, putting aside the overture, the music places one in an exceedingly difficult position ; for, while, like Byron's poem, it seems to make its true effect only when separated from the stage, it still needs to proceed step by step with the poem as it unfolds itself to the reader if he is to experience the illuminating aptness of the music to the inner meanings of the poem.

It would seem that despite Schumann's leaning towards stage presentation, his genius was essentially undramatic; for one fails to recall in his music, noble as is so much of it, and instinct with passion, one single vivid touch of drama. In the *Manfred* poem Schumann no doubt felt the reflection of the passionate melancholy that had, in fact, already begun to descend upon and to dominate his own mind; and it was probably that which inspired him, all unresisting, to illumine for us by the light of his own genius the glowing depths of Manfred's tortured soul.

Despite its unrelieved sombre colouring, the overture is probably the greatest piece of purely orchestral music Schumann ever achieved. It was first given in March, 1852, at Leipzig, when it made a deep impression, and when, if we can accept the opinion of his friend Pohl, he obtained from the orchestra a fine performance: " His manner was deeply serious; utterly absorbed in the music, oblivious of the audience and almost as much so of the players, he seemed to live the music and to *become* Manfred. I felt that this work, more than any other, was written with his heart's blood."

This production of the overture was followed by the staging of the complete work at Weimar in June, when Liszt conducted two performances ; but there seems to have been no other stage performance of the work within Schumann's lifetime.

There were several other compositions in this fruitful year : the *Album für die Jugend*, Opus 68, consists of some forty-three piano pieces of which he wrote to Karl Reinecke (October 1848) in Vienna : " I have asked from Schuberth (the Vienna publisher) fifty louis d'or. If you think it too much, let me know frankly." Schumann duly received his fifty louis d'or, and was as much pleased with the transaction, as with the little work, the composition of which had given him real pleasure. From a letter to K. Reinecke : " Of course one always loves the newest composition the most, but these pieces have wound themselves round my heart : I wrote the first five of them for our eldest daughter's birthday . . . . and you will find traces of the old humour in them. The point of view is quite different from the *Kinderscenen*, which were a grown person's recollections of childhood ; but these new pieces are the child's own ideas and imaginings of things and of future happenings."
The album quickly became popular and the publisher asked for another ; but an ordered

pendant scarcely came within Schumann's method of composition.

The other compositions of the year included the *Bilder aus Osten*, Opus 66, a set of charming piano duets :

Three Fantasiestücke for clarinet and piano, Opus 73 :

Adagio and Allegro for horn and piano, Opus 70 :

Requiem for Mignon, Opus 98B. from Goethe's *Wilhelm Meister*, a composition for voices and orchestra :

The *Advent Hymn*, Opus 71, for solo voice, chorus and orchestra : "I have turned my thoughts to the church," wrote Schumann ; "a small chorus was in my mind."

The first of the *Waldscenen*, Opus 82, was composed and the remainder of the set completed in the following year (1849).

In the spring of that year the prospect of a revolution in Dresden became so threatening that Schumann removed himself and his family to the village of Kreischa.

When the rising occurred, Dresden was no place for a sick man ; so, while the turbulent Wagner took a part that afterwards compelled him to fly secretly to Weimar, to Liszt (travelling on through Switzerland to the haven of Paris), Schumann, though feeling that the storms hard-by compelled him to work feverishly " to keep himself clear of their influence," continued his more peaceful avocation.

At Kreischa, surrounded by his children, he composed his *Lieder für die Jugend*, Opus 79. "You will see," he wrote, "that I have chosen poems from the greatest masters, but only those adapted to youth. You will also see how from simplicity I have passed to things more difficult, and they end with *Mignon* ' gazing with far-seeing eyes towards the spiritual life.' "

The other compositions either begun or completed at Kreischa included the

Spanisches Liederspiel, Opus 74 : a set of ten songs for four voices, of which Schumann wrote : " It is rather original in form, and as a whole has the happiest effect ;

The *Spanische Liebes-Lieder*, Opus 138 : a cycle of ten songs for several voices with four-handed piano accompaniment ;

and the *Concertstück for four horns and orchestra*, Opus 86. Schumann was anxious to produce this work at Leipzig, and wrote of it as " quite a curiosity," but the intended concert was abandoned.

The *Motet for double chorus* of male voices, Opus 93, originally had accompaniment for the organ, but later Schumann substituted an orchestral version :

New Year's Hymn, Opus 144, for chorus and orchestra, the poem being by Friedrich Rückert : and the *Introduction and Allegro* for piano and orchestra, Opus 92.

Throughout the term of the Schumanns' residence in Dresden, despite their ever increasing prestige, they made little or no progress in Court or official circles ; and though Schumann was never at his best at social functions, the fact of being ignored was galling to their pride.

After their return from Kreischa, Clara extended their social circle by instituting at their apartment a weekly gathering of musicians and other artists, when new works were produced, and a hearing given to those of unknown composers whom Schumann thought promising : it was, indeed, at one of their gatherings that Madam Schröder-Devrient first sang his *Spanisches Liederspiel.*

Learning in July from his Leipzig publisher, Dr. Härtel, that there was a probability of Rietz, the conductor of the Gewandhaus concerts, receiving a Berlin appointment, Schumann's love of the more congenial life of Leipzig reawakened ; and he lost no time in asking that his name be put forward unofficially as the possible successor. The rumour proved to be ill-founded, or at least premature ; but it sufficed to implant in Schumann's mind the idea of escaping from the restricted life of Dresden.

Later in the year news arrived from Ferdinand Hiller, at Düsseldorf, announcing his appointment to Köln, and inquiring whether Schumann would accept the Düsseldorf conductorship if it were offered. After much discussion of the pros and cons, Schumann wrote in November asking for definite information on many practical matters, adding: "Uppermost in my mind at the moment is Mendelssohn's opinion of music in Düsseldorf, and that was bad enough. When you accepted the post Rietz told me he could not understand how you could do so. . . . In any case I could not go before next Easter as my opera is to be performed at Leipzig in February, and I must be there."

December found him suffering greatly from headache, and from inflammation of the eyes that prevented his reading. Much depressed, he wrote to Hiller: "Though all you tell me inclines me to accept, I should much prefer to defer my final decision until Easter." He was still hoping to go to Leipzig in preference to Düsseldorf: "Looking up an old Geography book, I found among the chief buildings of the town, three convents and a lunatic asylum. This latter rather disconcerted me, for when we stayed at Maxen our apartment overlooked the local asylum, and it quite spoilt my visit. I should not like the same thing to happen again."

After a good deal of procrastination, the Gewandhaus being always at the back of his mind, to say nothing of efforts that were being made in other directions, and the success of which would have made him Capellmeister to the King of Saxony, Schumann eventually felt bound to accept Hiller's offer. It was therefore

arranged that he should take on his duties at
Düsseldorf in the next autumn (1850), drawing
his salary of 700 thalers a year from the beginning
of April.

During the year 1849 Schumann was much
perturbed by two deaths, that of his only
surviving brother Carl in April, and that of
Chopin in October. He proposed a memorial
service for Chopin at the *Frauenkirche*, but
officialdom declined it, to Schumann's intense
mortification.

Throughout the whole of the year Schumann
had been endeavouring to arrange for the
production of his opera *Genoveva*. A new
director had been appointed at the Leipzig
opera house at the beginning of the year, and
Schumann suggested that the airy promises of
the former management should then be reduced
to a contract, proposing a date in February for
the first performance. In February the date
was put back " a fortnight " ; but it was June
before the matter was advanced sufficiently for
Schumann to be asked to take up the rehearsals.
He was unable to do so, and the date for the
production was then put back till August. By
July the August date was cancelled, and Schumann
wrote to Dr. Härtel begging to be informed as
soon as anything was decided. In this way it
continued to drift until the following February
(1850), when, following upon the cancellation

of yet another date for the opera to be put into rehearsal, Schumann lost his temper. "It is hateful treatment; but I do not intend to allow them to fool me any longer." A few more months passed, and eventually the first perform-'ance took place on 25th June (1850).

There was a good attendance considering the season of the year, and Schumann conducted a performance that was fairly well received by the public. With the sole exception of Spohr, the more critical part of the audience generally condemned the work on the ground of monotony so that the opera was given only three performances. Some of the critiques in the press hit the composer very hard, indeed one written by Kruger, one of the regular contributors to the *Neue Zeitschrift*, gave him so much offence that he sent him a heated letter that brought their friendly correspondence to an abrupt end.

Bitterly disappointed at the reception of *Genoveva*, and contrasting it with the popular success achieved by *Le Prophete*, the work of his *bête noir*, Meyerbeer, Schumann set out with his wife on a concert tour through Bremen and Hamburg, where they gave a successful series of concerts.

On their return to Dresden preparations for the removal to Düsseldorf kept them fully occupied. Among others, the choral society gave them a farewell reception, but when with the 1st September came their departure, they quitted Dresden with few regrets, but with good hopes for their future happiness.

Schumann's six years at Dresden had been musically most prolific, and it was during this period that the development of his genius reached its highest point. Though variegated by numerous ups and downs both of health and of fortune, Schumann's Dresden period had been far from unprofitable. His music had at length begun to earn the recognition it deserved, and his position in his profession considerably improved.

Düsseldorf—The reception of the Schumanns—The first Concert—The *Rhenish Symphony*—*The Bride of Messina overture*—*Luther*—*The Pilgrimage of the Rose*—*Julius Cæsar overture*—*Der Königssohn*—*Des Sängers Fluch*—*Hermann und Dorothea overture*—*Rheinweinlied*—*D minor Violin Sonata*— *G minor Piano Trio*—Holiday in Switzerland—Adverse criticism—Schumann as conductor—The choral ballads—Choral *Nachtlied*—*Märchenbilder* for viola—The *Mass*—The *Requiem* —A Schumann Week in Leipzig—Ill-health—Scheveningen— Difficulties of the second concert season.

IN agreeable contrast with the official neglect they had experienced in Dresden, the reception of the Schumanns at Düsseldorf was distinguished by the utmost cordiality. On their arrival by *diligence* they were met by the concert directors, headed by Ferdinand Hiller who had been mainly responsible for the appointment of his successor. Formal presentations were made, and they were forthwith escorted by the whole party to the Breidenbacher Hof, the principal hotel of the city. Hiller had instilled into the musical section, both professional and amateur, a healthy enthusiasm, and a lively sense of the honour conferred upon Düsseldorf by the two distinguished musicians about to make it their home; and in the course of the first evening the gentlemen

of the Liedertafel serenaded them, while the
following night the town orchestra paid a similar
homage. A few days later the concert committee
gave an entertainment in their honour, consisting of a concert, followed by a supper and ball.
Out of compliment to Schumann the programme
of the concert was drawn entirely from his own
works ; viz., the overture to *Genoveva*, a group of
his songs, and the second part of *Paradise and
the Peri*. With such a successful beginning
everything appeared to the Schumanns *couleur de
rose*, and they turned with equanimity to the
problem of house-accommodation. This proved
less easy than they had anticipated. They found
Düsseldorf a city of delightful parks and pleasure
gardens, but with the knowledge that their
household goods and chattels would arrive only
five days after them, their hurried search for a
house led them to choose one in a district so
noisy that Schumann found it impossible to do
any work in it. There was therefore nothing
but to remove to other quarters, and this they
were compelled to do more than once.

Meanwhile Schumann lost no time in taking
up his new duties, which consisted in conducting
the orchestra and choir at the subscription
concerts, and various services in the Maximilian
Church ; with the preparatory work of training
and rehearsing both orchestra and chorus. He
found both of them in a state of high efficiency,
for they had the tradition of a series of capable

conductors, Mendelssohn, Julius Rietz, and Ferdinand Hiller. Within a month, moreover, Schumann brought von Wasielewski to Düsseldorf to become leader of the violins.

The first concert was given· on 24th October (1850) before an audience that overflowed the hall. A flourish of brass instruments greeted Schumann's arrival on the platform, and everybody was keyed-up to acclaim the genius.

The programme included Beethoven's *Weihe des Hauses* overture, Schumann's *Adventlied*, Gade's *Comala*, and Mendelssohn's *G Minor piano Concerto*, with the co-operation of Madame Schumann.

The concert was a success, but not a triumph ; for Schumann as conductor was not an inspiring leader, although Clara's note in the diary reads : " It was a great delight to me to see Robert conducting with a fine repose, and, when necessary, with splendid energy."

In short the Schumanns were well pleased with this *début ;* and though a considerable section of the cognoscenti was of two minds about the capabilities of the new conductor, the first series of concerts was so well supported that three additional concerts were given, at one of which Schumann ventured to present a programme chosen from the works of living composers, an unheard of thing in that day.

The reception of the Schumanns on the social side was no less enthusiastic than on the official side ; and they soon gathered about them a congenial circle of friends, of whom the leading figures were Wilhelm Schadow the principal of the Academy of Fine Arts, Hildebrandt the historical painter and musical enthusiast, von Wasielewski the violinist, and Julius Tausch the principal teacher of the piano in Düsseldorf, and conductor in the interregnum between Hiller and Schumann.

The neighbouring Cathedral city of Köln, a few miles up the Rhine, mightily impressed the Schumanns; and their first expedition to it furnished the inspiration for Schumann's *Rhenish Symphony*—the E flat, Opus 97, numbered III but actually composed some nine years later than the original version of the D minor, which when re-scored he numbered IV.

In the design of the *Rhenish Symphony* Schumann abandoned the classicism of the C major, and gave his romantic leanings full play. The work consists of five movements, the fourth of which was suggested to him by witnessing in Köln the imposing ceremony attendant upon the election of an Archbishop to the Cardinalate. He marked this movement: *In the style of music incidental to a solemn ceremony*; and it is certainly an unusual type of movement to form part of a symphony.

Schumann conducted his *Rhenish Symphony* at Düsseldorf early in the following February (1851) and at Köln at the end of the same month; but despite the fact of its scherzo being a singularly poetic movement, instinct with the romanticism associated with the Rhine in the heart of all good Germans, the work created little impression on either occasion.

Soon after the transfer to Düsseldorf, Richard Pohl, then a student of natural history at Leipzig, submitted an opera libretto based upon Schiller's *Braut von Messina* ; and, " after reading it several times," Schumann wrote to Pohl, " I found in it the idea for an overture, and I have, in fact, already composed it." The overture to *The Bride of Messina*, Opus 100, was performed at the Gewandhaus, Leipzig, in November (1851), but was received with little enthusiasm. " Have you heard the overture ? " he wrote to Pohl ; " I hear various accounts of the effect it makes ; but I am quite used by now to the public not understanding my works at a first hearing, especially the better ones."

From the time of the production of his first group of *Scenes from Faust*, Schumann had become more and more receptive of the religious idea. We have already noted, even before the $E\flat$ *Symphony*, the *Advent-hymn* (of 1848), the great *Motet for double chorus* and the *New Year's Hymn* (1849). In January (1851) he wrote to Richard Pohl at Leipzig that he was ready to compose an oratorio, and perhaps on the subject Luther or Ziska (the leader of the Hussites in the fourteenth century), or on some subject from the Bible.

Pohl responded with preliminary sketches for a Gargantuan oratorio, *Luther*, designed as a trilogy. " It is so tremendous a subject," wrote Schumann, " that we must eliminate everything not absolutely necessary for its development. Three evenings would be too much : let us say one evening of two hours and a half," and suggested his taking Händel's *Israel in Egypt* as a model for designing the choral part of this work.

Much correspondence ensued, but by the end of the year Schumann began to doubt " whether after all we shall ever master the subject." At the end of the following year he wrote : " Luther is still dormant." At the end of 1853 he returned him to the author, and dormant he has ever since remained.

But Schumann was meanwhile far from dormant, and for a rather trivial fairy poem that Moritz Horn of Chemnitz sent him, *The Pilgrimage of the Rose*, he composed the music between April and July (1851), Opus 112. He designed the work for solo voices, chorus, and piano, " sufficient accompaniment for so delicate a subject," though he afterwards added orchestra. The music absorbed into itself some of the sentimentality that overflowed the poem, which indeed contained nothing worthy of the elaborate musical means employed ; yet after the production Schumann wrote to Dr. Klitzsch that " it made a very agreeable impression on the audience.

Both in form and in manner it is like the *Peri*, but more rustic, more German."

In May (1851) Schumann wrote to Moritz Hauptmann: "Here by the Rhine there is almost more music than in Central Germany. The Musical Festivals have increased the demands of the public in an extraordinary way; and I like it thus, for it is more agreeable to *keep* people up to a high standard than to *force* them up to it." In the same month he wrote to Hauptmann: "I have just composed an overture to Shakespeare's play, *Julius Cæsar*; it will reach you later on." In June he composed *Der Königssohn*, Opus 116, using Uhland's dramatic ballad, for solo voices, chorus, and orchestra, and at once consulted Pohl about finding something further of the same genre. "It strikes me that there are many German ballads that could be treated musically as concert pieces for voices and orchestra. First of all I have in mind Uhland's *Des Sängers Fluch*; though it would have to be moulded in a few places to meet my musical requirements. Have you time to do it?" At the beginning of December Pohl sent the text finally corrected, and by mid-January (1852) Schumann wrote: "The composition is all sketched, but the orchestration remains to be done." This was completed as Opus 139, but a year later the production was still held up for want of a good harpist.

At Christmas (still 1851) he composed an overture to Goethe's *Hermann und Dorothea*, Opus 136, on which he thought of basing an operetta. Difficulties intervened, and he consulted Horn, the author of *The Pilgrimage of the Rose*, about making it into a cantata. That fell through too, so nothing more than the overture was composed.

To this period also belong the *Rheinweinlied*, a festival overture with solo voices and chorus, Opus 123; the *Sonata in D minor for Violin and Piano*, Opus 121, and the *Pianoforte Trio in G minor*, Opus 110. This is the last of the three trios that he composed; but it is scarcely worthy of being ranked with the other two, belonging, as they do, to his finest chamber music period. But in sending the trio to his publisher, Schumann wrote : " I have now put the finishing touches. We heard it played two days ago, and it went splendidly; I thought to myself, ' Now you can send it out into the world! ' You are to pay me the same for it as for the piano quintet, as a trio can count on a far larger sale than a quintet."

In July the Schumanns went by way of Heidelberg to Switzerland for a holiday; and in the middle of August Robert visited Antwerp, where he had been invited to adjudicate at the musical festival of the Männergesangverein.

In August he wrote to Klitzsch : " I am well

content with my position at Düsseldorf. It does not tax my strength too much, for though conducting always tires me, I like nothing better." And again, to Moscheles : " There is a great deal done here to promote good music, and I often congratulate myself on having found a sphere of action which so nearly corresponds to my desires."

Schumann was evidently oblivious of there being anything amiss between himself and his Düsseldorf musical public ; or, sensitive to adverse criticism as he undoubtedly was, he would scarcely have been writing in so happy a frame of mind. We have seen that his first series of concerts (1850-51) had been well attended ; but at its end an article appeared in the local press judging and condemning Schumann as a conductor. Now Schumann believed himself a capable conductor ; while, whether as conductor or composer, Clara thought him little less than a god. Such an article, therefore, while regarded by them as an impertinence, aroused in neither of them any suspicion that the criticism might be well founded. The affront caused them nothing more than a momentary pang, for they attributed it to one of the members of the concert direction whom they regarded as inimical.

But the trouble was far deeper rooted than they imagined, for the musical public, who had welcomed Schumann with so much effusion, had soon become dubious of his powers as a conductor ; and when they finally recognized the extent by which the great man fell short of their expectations, very humanly attributed to him the blame for their own mistake.

When rehearsals were resumed in September, the demeanour of the choir at once betrayed their lack of enthusiasm. The attendance was poor, discipline began to vanish, and Schumann himself noted in his diary : " The choir is not what it was, no enthusiasm, no ardour." He was out of touch with it; instead of having the choir more in hand in his second season, it was the contrary, and friction naturally began to appear. Schumann's manner, retiring, aloof, was not what the choir had been accustomed to, nor was it what any choir needs to inspire it with confidence. Their performances suffered ; they knew it ; and they blamed Schumann, little realizing that the increasing hesitancy in his speech, and what appeared to them to be apathy, marked in reality some fresh stride in the fell malady that overhung him. Towards the end of the season, however, Schumann conducted his *B♭ Symphony* with outstanding success, and for the moment his unsuitability as a conductor was forgotten in the enthusiasm aroused by the composer.

Early in this season (1851-2) Schumann founded a chamber music society, and also a singing club. But here again his method of

conducting did not suffice to hold the attention
either of audience, or singers, and Madame
Schumann in particular was greatly incensed at
their inattention and chattering.

The concert season ran its length; but
although there was no open mutiny, it was
recognized by everybody, except the Schumanns,
that a change would have to be made before the
next season. Madame Schumann indeed complained bitterly that the directors took no
active steps " to shield her husband in every
way in order not to lose him."

At the season's end, she said she would be glad
if he withdrew from the conductorship of the
choir, " such a position being unworthy of him ";
but neither of them seriously contemplated the
possibility of any such step so long as he remained
at Düsseldorf.

In May (1852) Schumann wrote to a friend in
Vienna : " Something in Vienna seems to draw
me to it again, as though the spirits of the great
dead could still be felt there, in what is really
the home of German music. It is not impossible
that we shall come to Vienna again, indeed I am
much inclined to."

Notwithstanding his desire to beat an honorable
retreat, he still continued to work industriously
at composition, chiefly of choral works :

The *Vom Pagen und der Königstochter*, Opus
140, consists of four ballads by Geibel ; and

Das Glück von Edenhall, Opus 143, is the ballad

by Uhland; and although one and all of
Schumann's choral ballads reveal his striving
after the dramatic in music, it was an ideal that
he never really succeeded in capturing.

The choral *Nachtlied*, Opus 108, was a setting
of a poem by Friedrich Hebbel. Schumann wrote
that he aimed at the production of the dark
colour he felt the poem needed, and this is,
probably, the first instance of a chorus being
used to share in the production of effects purely
orchestral that undoubtedly contributed to the
composer's more complete re-utterance of the
phantasy of the poem.

The other compositions of this period include
the *Märchenbilder for Viola and Piano*, Opus 113,
containing mostly gloomy music such as, knowing
the state of his mind, might have been expected.

Neither his *Mass*, Opus 147, nor the *Requiem*,
Opus 149, can be properly described as church
music, as they depart both in form and content
from the demands of the church ritual; and as
he cannot but have been aware of this, he
probably intended them only for concert
performances.

The *Mass* is a noble work, containing as it
does some of Schumann's finest writing for
chorus, and may be classed among his highest
achievements.

" A *Requiem*," wrote he, " is one of the things
one composes for oneself alone "; and that
remark applies also to a considerable proportion

of Schumann's music. The subject is one that might have been expected to inspire his genius, and one can only attribute to the known state of his health the comparative failure of this, almost his last big work.

In March (1852) the Schumanns visited Leipzig, when a " Schumann week " was held in his honour. The programme included the *Manfred* overture, the *E♭ Symphony*, the *Pilgrimage of the Rose* and the *Piano trio in G minor*; while there was also a private performance of the *D minor Sonato for Violin and Piano*.

In the following August Schumann conducted part of the Festival of music for male voices at Düsseldorf, but his ill-health prevented his taking a very strenuous part ; and after the effort Madame Schumann took him to Scheveningen for a rest until mid-September. " Perhaps the good fairies will give me back my strength," he wrote from there ; but the success of the holiday was spoilt by Madame Schumann falling ill too.

After the return to Düsseldorf : " we have been through much worry and sickness, but things are rather brighter." But he admitted to nervous irritability remaining, " so have to be extremely moderate with all brain work. I wish I could go to Vienna as conductor, if only a post were open." He had already written to Sonderhausen where he heard there was likely to be a vacancy ; and also proposed to Julius Stern in Berlin an exchange of posts. This apparent restlessness was no doubt attributable to his recognition of the air of unfriendliness on his return to Düsseldorf.

The reception of the Schumanns at the first of the new season's concerts was markedly cold, and to the sensitive man the fact of all the preparations for the concert having been completed in his absence (though of course necessarily) appeared as an affront.

The feeling of the choir at that time may be gauged by the fact that three of its committee waited on Schumann with the proposal that, as he was unable to fulfil his duties, he should forthwith resign. Tausch was supposed to be behind the malcontents, but had Schumann possessed anything of the tenacity and the pugnacity of a Wagner, he might perhaps have held the field in spite of them. But he was of a different mould, and though capable of a momentary ebullition through pique, his chief tenacity was the tenacity of self-restraint.

Apology was of course forthcoming, for the maladroit move of the three committee-men ; but the atmosphere remained thunderous, and throughout the season the movement in favour of Tausch contrived to gather strength, its course made easy by Schumann's increasing ineffectiveness as a conductor.

Ill-health—The Lower Rhine Festival—*Schön Hedwig—Faust Overture—Concertstück for piano and orchestra—Fantasie and concerto for violin—'Cello concerto*—Last pieces for violin, piano and clarinet—Johannes Brahms—Ideas of leaving Düsseldorf—Schumann's position there—The re-arrangement of his duties—Concert tour in Holland—Literary work—The *Gesammelte · Schriften—Dichtergarten für Musik*—His health gives way—His removal to Endenich—-Hope abandoned—The end.

As the musical season drifted into the New Year (1853) Schumann became ill again, and though not sufficiently so to prevent him working, it was obvious that it would be impossible for him to conduct the whole of the Spring Festival of the Lower Rhine, to be held in Düsseldorf. " I suppose you will agree to my conducting the *Messiah* and my Symphony," he wrote to Hiller, who had been invited to come ; and it was also agreed that Julius Tausch should share the task of conducting. That the Committee had unshaken confidence in Schumann as a composer is shown by three of his important works being included in the festival programme. They were the Festival overture, *Rheinweinlied* with chorus and solo voices, the *Pianoforte Concerto in A minor*, and his revised version of the *D minor Symphony*, which in particular made a deep impression : " When we last heard that Symphony, at Leipzig," wrote Schumann, to Verhulst, " I never thought it would reappear on such an occasion as this. I was against its being included, but was persuaded by some of the Committee who had heard it. I have scored it afresh, and it is now more effective."

His compositions of this year include : *Schön Hedwig*, Opus 106, for pianoforte. " I have not set Hebbel's poem to music, but have made incidental music for it—quite a peculiar effect," wrote Schumann.

In the autumn he wrote to Joachim : " It has come to pass as you prophesied, for I have at last composed an overture to my *Scenes from Faust*." In another letter he writes of the overture as putting " the finishing touch " to the whole work ; but the addition was unfortunately scarcely on the level of either of its three parts. It was, in effect, an after-thought that occurred so long after the event that the original inspiration was dead.

Other works of the summer were the

Concertstück for Piano and Orchestra, Opus 134.

A Fantasie for Violin and Orchestra, Opus 131, which he composed for Joachim ;

A *Concerto for Violin and Orchestra*, also for Joachim, to whom he wrote : " This is easier than the *Fantasie*, and there is, too, more for the orchestra to do "; but the work has never been published.

There was also a Concerto for *Violoncello and Orchestra*, Opus 129, with a slow movement of notable beauty.

Of the *Violin Sonata in D minor*, Opus 121, which followed, he wrote to Joachim : " You were often in my mind as I wrote it, and that encouraged me ; tell me of anything in it you consider too difficult to play, for I have often given you unpalatable dishes, or at any rate mouthfuls. Strike out anything unplayable."

Beyond these there were :

Four pieces for Clarinet, Viola and Piano, under the title of *Märchenerzählungen*, Opus 132 ;

Three piano Sonatas for the Young, Opus 118 ;

And a set of Six piano pieces for four hands, issued with the title *Kinderball*, Opus 130.

In the autumn Johannes Brahms, then twenty years of age, and quite unknown, visited Düsseldorf, with introductions from Joseph Joachim, the violinist. Schumann wrote to his publisher, Dr. Härtel : " A young man has appeared here, and impressed us all with his wonderful music. I am convinced he will make a great name."

Within a few days he wrote an in-seeing essay on Brahms, and, after reading it to a select circle of friends, dispatched it to the *Neue Zeitschrift für Musik* in Leipzig for publication.

Brahms stayed about a month in Düsseldorf, constantly making music with the Schumanns, and, when he left, he was provided by Robert with a flattering introduction to his own publishers. Schumann pressed him to make the journey to Leipzig to see them, and take with them his string quartet, Op. 1 ; two books of songs, Op. 2 and Op. 4 ; his Scherzo, Op. 3 ; and his piano sonata, Opus 5. " And we must not forget to deal with the prosaic part as well : I have asked for them forty Friedrich's d'or, and think that would be a fair beginning." The introduction was a complete success, and Schumann was greatly rejoiced, as indeed was Joachim, their mutual friend. A little later Schumann wrote to Joachim : " I like the cigars much ; there is something Brahmsian about them, rather strong, but full of flavour. They make me think of his cheery smile."

In another letter to Joachim, however, we find a reference to a more serious matter : " We shall soon be leaving Düsseldorf altogether. I have had it on my mind for a long time ; but am now decided. We are sick of the snobs here ; but all this is only for your ear and Brahms'."

In another letter of the same time he writes : " We intend to cut ourselves loose from this by the winter after next (1854-5) and shall probably move to Vienna. Life in a small town no longer suits us ; it is nothing but endless repetition, the result of moving in a circle."

It is obvious that Schumann's position in Düsseldorf must by now have become one of extreme delicacy. He had undertaken duties that he was both physically and temperamentally incapable of fulfilling, and being quite unable to realize the fact, could only attribute to an evil cabal the signs of discontent that could not but make themselves felt with increasing frequency. The orchestra, the choir and the concert committee, however, all felt that Schumann was in his wrong place, and were agreed that some step must be taken. But what step ? Schumann had been ill in February, and again in July, and it was obvious to all, when the rehearsals were resumed in the autumn, that the conductor was less than ever fit for his work. It was remarked that his bodily movements seemed slow and difficult, and his speech heavy and laboured. He seemed incapable of indicating quick *tempi*, and his manner at the conductor's desk was increasingly strange and vacant. On one occasion, when about to begin a Symphony he remained motionless, with raised *bâton*, apparently lost in dreams, and he was only brought back to the surrounding realities by Joachim, who was leading the violins, taking the initiative and starting the movement. At one celebration of mass he was seen to continue to beat time absent-mindedly long after the movement had ended, and after the priest had begun intoning.

On another occasion the Church performance was so bad as to create something approaching a public scandal, and at length it became clear, even to a Committee, that it had to deal with a sick man.

It was, therefore, suggested to Schumann that in view of his ill-health, he should agree to conduct none but his own works, leaving the deputy conductor, Julius Tausch, to take the rest of the work.

Schumann construed this offer as a deliberate affront; sent no reply; but left his deputy to take the next rehearsal, and as the Committee decided that the deputy should, in the circumstances, also conduct the concert, Schumann from that time ceased to act as Music Director. From Madame Schumann's notes in the diary, one sees that she was desperately biassed against the unfortunate deputy conductor: "Robert has told the Committee he will conduct no more," writes she on 9th November; "Tausch is behaving like the unmannerly boor that he is. . . He ought to refuse to conduct, as Robert told him. . . ."

Schuman had indeed written to Tausch: "If you conduct to-day, I cannot regard you as treating me fairly."

Clara's entry continues: "It is quite clear that Tausch has been at the bottom of the whole intrigue." Again on November 10th: "This is the Concert evening, and here we sit at home while Tausch conducts the concert. Robert has sent him a letter to-day that he would not be proud to show."

Poor Tausch was always, after that time, roundly abused by Madame Schumann for what she believed to be " his share in the intrigue," but she was prejudiced against him from the first. An earlier entry in her diary : " Tausch conducted quite well. But it is a pity he is not personally more agreeable ; there is something in his face I do not like."

Nevertheless there is no proof that he acted in any way dishonourably, and, indeed, he had a great respect for Schumann ; but the fact of his being well-known in Düsseldorf long before Schumann arrived there, and of his being an efficient conductor, who had constantly acted as deputy, made him the first man for the Committee to turn to in their exceedingly awkward dilemma.

Their contract with Schumann had been drawn to terminate at the middle of 1854 ; and the agreement they now made with Tausch was for him to act as deputy, conducting all but the most important works, those being set aside to be conducted by the Music Director, who still retained his appointment, an arrangement, be it said, by no means ungenerous to Schumann.

Professor Wieck, who knew Tausch personally, has described him as " a taciturn man without the gift of smooth speech " ; but he had been recommended to Düsseldorf by Mendelssohn, and Professor Niecks knew him as a good musician, and an experienced conductor. Schumann himself said as much in his early days at Düsseldorf, and, until the catastrophe, certainly bore him no ill-will; indeed after rehearsal it was the custom of the two to adjourn to a neighbouring café and divide a small bottle of champagne.

In November and December the Schumanns undertook a concert tour in Holland, giving concerts together in Amsterdam, Rotterdam, Scheveningen, Utrecht and the Hague. Clara achieved even more than her customary successes, and Robert was delighted to find his works well prepared for him : " At Rotterdam and Utrecht the *Third Symphony*, at Amsterdam and the Hague the *Second Symphony*, the *Pilgrimage of the Rose* at the Hague, so that I had only to stand up and conduct."

Schumann arrived home in Düsseldorf early in January, and immediately plunged into literary work. From a letter of 17th January, 1854 : " Encouraged by a Leipsig publisher I had long determined in my mind to re-edit my Essays on music and literature." From his letter proposing the publication to Dr. Härtel : " I have a peculiar proposal for you. You are to become my literary publisher. When re-reading some old volumes of my *Zeitschrift*, I became quite absorbed. The whole period, down to the time when Mendelssohn reached his zenith, unfolded itself to me as I read. Then it flashed upon me that I would collect these scattered leaves, for they make life-like pictures of an interesting period and are full of helpful hints."

Dr. Härtel declined the idea of a literary publication at the time, but some thirty years afterwards purchased the copyright of the work, the *Gesammelte Schriften*, which was published by Wigand of Leipzig in four volumes, priced at a hundred thalers.

The essays have since been translated into English by Miss Fanny Ritter, and published by W. Reeves.

The re-editing of these papers occupied Schumann for the whole January following upon his return from Holland, broken only by a visit to Hanover, where Joachim conducted Schumann's *Fourth Symphony*, and played the *Fantasie for Violin*. There the reunion of the trio, Schumann, Joachim and Brahms, was a source of pleasure to all of them : " very merry ; great consumption of champagne," says the diary.

With energy apparently undiminished, Schumann signalled his arrival home from Hanover by launching out upon even another literary project, no less than a poetical anthology on the subject of music, under the title of the *Dichtergarten für Musik* (the Poet's Garden of Music). On the 6th February (1854) he wrote to Joachim : " Music here is silent just now ; but my *Dichtergarten* is growing apace and looks more and more splendid. I am setting up sign-posts here and there, so that people shall not lose their way—of course, these might be called just explanatory notes. I have delved into the ancients, Homer and Plato, and have collected some glorious passages."

At a later date, when he was beyond such work, he wrote to a friend that he had intended the anthology to show the effect of music upon the poets. " The noblest and finest would have come from the works of Luther, Shakespeare, Jean Paul and Rückert. From their works my first part would have been drawn : the second from the Holy Scriptures. . . . Jesus, the son of Sirach, utters some fine things :

" Hinder not music.
 Pour not out talk when there is a performance of music.
 And display not thy wisdom out of season.
 As a signet of carbuncle in a setting of gold,
 So is a concert of music in a banquet of wine.
 As a signet of emerald in a work of gold,
 So is a strain of music with pleasant wine."

Schumann worked at this anthology with hectic energy, that reminds one of his father's feat of writing seven novels within two years. Though characteristic of Schumann's usual mode of work, there seemed in this case to be something uncanny about it, that filled his wife with an anxiety, unhappily only too well founded. For within ten days of this return home, Schumann was taken ill, alarmingly so ; " acute and painful auditory affection," is the note in the diary. The symptoms developed quickly during the next week, and intense melancholia settled upon him, accompanied by delusions, the supposed appearance of good and evil spirits ; he imagined Schubert and Mendelssohn appearing before him, bringing him musical themes. Clara never left him and it is from her that we learn that one day about the end of the month, he collected with perfect calmness, some manuscripts and clothes that he said he would require in an asylum, and implored his wife to take him to one at once.

Soothed by her gentleness, he slept until the next morning, when he returned to his work at some piano variations that he had in hand.

His little daughter, Marie, was sitting with him—Clara being in consultation with the doctor—when he suddenly rose, moaning, and though only partially dressed, left the house. Heavy rain was falling at the time and when the child gave the alarm he had disappeared. The whole household searched in vain for him, and it was two hours before he was brought home by people who had rescued him from the river into which he had flung himself.

The next week he was removed to a private asylum at Endenich, not far from Bonn (4th March, 1854).

Even there he worked from time to time at composition and put finishing touches to a book of *Romances for Violoncello and Piano*, Opus 94, and another for piano alone, *Gesänge der Frühe* (Morning Songs), Opus 126, being seven pieces in fughetta form.

He also wrote there some piano accompaniments for the Paganini studies, and made more variations on the themes that he imagined emanated from Schubert. From a letter: " My beloved wife contrives with letters and news of her musical activities, to send sweet cheer into my solitude ; there was news of Brahms' doings—his genius delving to the depths of musical utterance, or transfigured to its heights ; of Joachim, the wizard, with a creative power even surpassing his virtuosity."

At such times it seemed not impossible that he should recover, and in his less disturbed intervals he was able to receive visits from Brahms, Joachim, and other intimate friends ; but by the autumn of the next year (1855) all hope of recovery was abandoned.

He still carried on an intermittent correspondence, but his spirit was gradually failing.

In the spring of 1856, Madame Schumann had to undertake a concert tour in England, and on her return, in July, learned that it was impossible for Robert to live more than a few months or even weeks.

On the 23rd she was notified that a crisis had occurred, and she went post haste to Endenich. She was dissuaded from seeing her husband, and induced to return home. This was more than she could endure, however, and she went back to Endenich four days later. Accompanied by Johannes Brahms she visited her husband the same evening, but though they found him incapable of speaking intelligently, he was not beyond recognizing them.

Clara spent the whole of the next day with him, when he appeared to her to be conversing though half inaudibly, with imaginary beings around him. Brahms shared her vigil of the ensuing night, and on the following day (29th July, 1856) the sufferer passed peacefully away in his sleep, about four in the afternoon.

On the same day arrived Joachim from Heidelberg; and two days later he attended the simple ceremony of the funeral at Bonn, accompanied by Brahms and Ferdinand Hiller, the three most intimate friends of one of the most poetic composers of his century.

Chapter XVI

In following the course of the development of Schumann's genius, it will have been observed that to each of the successive periods of his life falls a group of compositions of a certain definite type, at first to the complete exclusion of all others, an exclusion that relaxed by gentle degrees.

His first period gave us only pianoforte compositions; then followed the year of songs with pianoforte accompaniments; then came the chamber music, which with the exception of the three string quartets, chiefly centred round the piano.

The piano concerto falls within the period of the symphonies that overlapped that of the chamber music to some extent. The symphonies are spread over a wider period, into which came the choral works with orchestra, beginning with *Paradise and the Peri*, and followed later by *Scenes from Faust*; then his contrapuntal period; then the opera, *Genoveva*, and other stage works, such as *Manfred*; the Choral Ballads; the separate Overtures, beginning with *The Bride of Messina*; and finally the *Motet*, the *Mass*, and the *Requiem*.

Schumann was a rapid writer, and the routine of his daily life in what was almost its most productive period, makes it clear that he was also an industrious one. At that time in Dresden, he worked uninterruptedly each morning—after lunch a walk with his wife—then work again until six o'clock, when he put it aside for the day, and walked round to a neighbouring restaurant, where he read the newspapers, and possibly met a few friends. But it was more usual with him to choose a table away from the chattering crowd ; and then he would place himself, with his back to them, frequently whistling to himself and probably developing his ideas in an imaginary world far removed from his surroundings. He invariably returned home to supper at eight o'clock ; after which early to bed—a methodical day.

All his earlier works were composed sitting at the pianoforte by way of improvization for which from childhood he had an extraordinary facility. And it was not until much later that he recognized the desirability of freeing himself from the limitations that such a method imposed upon the creation of any other than pianoforte music. But now, having realized this, he frequently impressed it upon his correspondents. From a letter of May, 1852 : " Do not fail to make a practice of *imagining* your music in your own mind without the assistance of the piano. Only in that way will you ever give free expression to the fount of your emotions. This is not a subject that one can write much about; but the chief thing is that the composer should *keep clear the ear of his mind.*"

Schumann was a great student of counterpoint; but, unlike many students of this subject, sought the soul in it, instead of resting satisfied with its external formal development. For the musician the art of counterpoint is one that has an irresistible fascination, each finding in it only what he seeks; while its technique naturally varies according to the *genre* of the themes, subjects, or melodies, of which it is composed or is to be composed.

The handling of the older counterpoint is not unlike the building of an harmonious device, with blocks of various shapes and of various colours, but each of them of unrelenting rigidity. A later type of counterpoint comes nearer to resembling a tapestry, stitched with snippets of movement (moving parts) that emerge and disappear like so many varicoloured strands, which when woven in just combination, make up an organized whole.

A still later and more plastic genre of counterpoint is more like loose strands of colour, or of coloured light, streaming onwards towards the same ultimate goal, " speaking each other in passing " if you will, but reaching it by different and more or less independent routes.

This last phase is the growth of a day later than Schumann's, and the counterpoint that claimed his attention, was that of Johann Sebastian Bach, in which, contrary to the musical experience of his day, he found the great soul that gave it animation. From the time of his studies of Bach the spirit of counterpoint permeated his conception of the art of composition; yet the species of counterpoint that he made his own was no mere imitation of the past, but rather a personal art, developed by the re-action of the spirit of all the counterpoint of the past upon his own musical ideas and upon his need of expressing them.

If one may hazard a characterization of the counterpoint of the four masters who influenced Schumann, then Bach's counterpoint was fundamental, Händel's victorious, Beethoven's elemental, and Schubert's intuitive. But Schumann's was none of these, being of a type singularly personal to himself, persuasive, caressive, and, unlike himself, conversational; and if one may borrow an analogy from the sister art of painting, there is something in the way in which Schumann handled his counterpoint that reminds one of the subtle use of colours in John MacNeil Whistler's arrangements.

Apart from the pianoforte, instrumental colour is a musical sense in which Schumann was curiously lacking; indeed, his orchestral music seems to have been originally imagined in terms of the piano. Almost every score of his chamber music and of his orchestral music had, after performance, to undergo a tedious course of correction and revision, although in it Schumann was making no excursions for the discovery of new instrumental effects. His instrumentation was scarcely abreast of its development in his day. and he was content mainly to rely upon a few orchestral formulæ, while Berlioz, across the border, was finding out how to make his music iridescent, and Richard Wagner, hard by, was giving new meanings to instrumental colour; yet the colour sense of those two composers differed not a jot less than do the brushwork of a Rembrandt and a Pater, or of a Monticelli and a Turner who with a brushful of paint could make, not a bit of blue, but a bit of heaven.

It almost seems that as long as Schumann knew that a passage was playable by an instrument, he was satisfied to write it. As a simple example of this misconception, the harp accompaniments to the three Hebrew melodies in Opus 95, are not harp music but pianoforte music that *could* be played upon the harp, without, however, evoking the special beauties of the instrument. Not unnaturally orchestral players were prejudiced against such treatment of their beloved instruments, and probably showed it.

From a letter to his publishers about one of his orchestral compositions : " I am glad to get it performed by the gentlemen of the orchestra, who taste a new composition as if it were a sour apple."

236

What we know as musical style cannot exist where the medium to be used is not completely suitable and its idiosyncrasies thoroughly understood and met ; hence Schumann's purely orchestral music is generally less successful as a work of art than is his pianoforte music, for in that he is never at fault.

In his songs he occasionally achieved a wonderful thing ; and that he did by some act of genius explainable by no logic ; for until his year of song, he had thought little of songs, and of the voice not at all. If then there is an explanation of his song successes, for he must, of course, be judged only by his best, it is that being, as he was, deeply, ecstatically in love, and accepting in that happy state every love poem that he found as an expression of his own ecstasy, he was impelled by the glow within him to give it re-utterance in a musical medium with which he had little familiarity. It is, therefore, little surprising that while in his songs the pianoforte accompaniments are of endless variety, his vocal line exhibits a tendency to repeat itself.

The pianoforte was his first instrument, and his best. He plumbed its possibilities to their depths, and in writing for this instrument he was able to express himself without the struggles that other instruments cost him ; he had to call in the assistance of no other to decide what passage was graceful or suitable as was the case when dealing with other instruments.

It is in his pianoforte compositions, and the works in which the piano bears an important part, such as the *Concerto in A minor*, the piano quintet, the piano quartet, and the first two of the three trios, that Schumann best expresses all that was best and greatest in himself, often with something of the fanciful humour that was also one of the characteristics of his literary work. This is often embodied in a delightful animation that is quite irresistible, and is found, too, not less often in his more romantic pieces.

His earlier works abound in melodic fragments, rather than in melodies, and it was one of his triumphs to be able to express, in so little a space, ideas of an elevated beauty that sings on in the heart long after the impression of the pianist faded. The idea of virtuoso-music was antipathetic to him, and he disliked it in others too. From a letter to a fellow composer : " Every now and again I find the *pianist* within you too much *en evidence* in your music ; but if you aim at anything beyond merely ephemeral effect, you must pitch him overboard, for only that which is inspired from within will hold its own."

Schumann's elaborate titles to his piano pieces, and sets of pieces, were, he frequently asserted in his correspondence, invariably added after the compositions were completed ; but he apparently considered that they still needed just the addition of such suggestive titles to bring the hearer into a state of mind corresponding to that which had been his when composing the pieces.

Though in his larger works Schumann inclined towards the accepted Germanic ideal of structural balance, of architecture, in his more intimate piano music that probably best enabled him to express himself, he allowed himself an imaginative freedom that bore him on strong pinions beyond any boundaries that for the moment seemed to impede his flight into the realms of romance that lay, after all, so near to his heart.

CHAPTER XVII

IN any attempt to sum up the contradictions of such a man as Robert Schumann, one cannot but find oneself face to face with a score of irreconcilable traits incident to his peculiar genius, with traits thrice loveable, and with others quite unworthy. The resulting discomfort of mind forces one to seek a solution of the difficulty by remembering that such contradiction to his actions as is offered by his letters, suggests a hyper-sensitive man whose conception alike of things and of the happenings about him, came to him through senses that were coloured or stained according to the state of his health at the moment.

As a young man we have seen him a self-indulgent poseur, affecting to see in himself one of the pain-racked heroes of his poet-hero of the hour—Lord Byron; not Byron's Corsair, but his Manfred, or perhaps his Werner. From this unpromising material, it would almost seem that something of a miracle was needed to make of it the great-souled loveable man we know him to have become. " Les choses humaines n'inspirent que deux sentiments aux esprits bien faits : l'admiration où la pitié," wrote Anatole

240

France; but, though we pity the follies, we realize none the less the necessity for the miracle; but where seek it ?

The unimaginable touch of time, and the great love of a responsive woman—these sufficed, and the miracle happened.

Schumann was above the middle height and carried his well-built figure well. In middle life his personal appearance reflected something of the nobility of his mind : his eyes were especially kindly, and his rather full lips had a pursed-up look suggestive of whistling. With the advance of years, his manner of walking has been described as giving the appearance of his having no bones in his body, and at that time he frequently moved about as one in a dream, utterly oblivious of his surroundings. His ill-health has played so unhappy a part throughout his life as I have recounted it, that it is only now necessary to draw a conclusion that from a comparatively early date, Schumann was aware that he could not count upon his brain to serve him for the full span of a life. At the age of twenty-seven he wrote : " I often feel that I shall not live much longer." His family was no long-lived one ; his father died at fifty-three, his brother Julius at twenty-eight, Edouard at forty-two, and there was always the memory of his unhappy sister Emilie who drowned herself at nineteen.

When his health allowed of it, he could become

buoyant, and his natural pluck forced him to go on with his work ill or no. There is a pathetic little passage from a letter of 1849 indicating his doubt of the future: " I have worked at high pressure all this year as you know ; for *one is bound to work as long as the daylight lasts.*"

Schumann was deeply interested in the work of his contemporaries, and indeed regarded a self-centred artist as lost. As his fame extended he was approached by many composers for advice and help, and to these he gave ungrudgingly but with a fine discrimination. From a letter to J. G. Herzog (1842) : " Do not write too many *little things:* try your hand at something bigger such as a fugue, or toccata. And write for the *voice.* That gets you on more than anything, and brings out the innermost qualities of the musician."

He was quick to express his admiration of his friends and of their work, and never tired of lauding Bach to the skies. His musical taste was eclectic; and he was not afraid to praise wholeheartedly. Thus in a letter to F. Brendel, July 1818 : " Palestrina's music is like the music of the spheres : and what art ! He is Italy's greatest musical genius of all time."

" Franz Schubert," wrote Schumann, " was, after Beethoven, the greatest master who made music his vocation in the noblest sense of the word."

Of Weber's Euryanthe:

"It is his heart's blood, and the very best of it. It cost him a piece of his life, but he gave it willingly, and it has immortalized him. From beginning to end it is a chain of the purest gems."

Of Chopin, he wrote in his *Neue Zeitschrift*, as the "finest and proudest poetic spirit of the time."

Of Mendelssohn he wrote with enthusiasm, and was perhaps the only one of his composer-idolators who did not also become one of his imitators.

Schumann was in some ways ahead of his time in his musical appreciation, but could lay about him with a vigour when he thought it necessary, or damn with an air of patronage in the best critical manner: From a letter to Kossmaly, of January, 1842:

"On the whole Marschner quite deserves a little distinction, and I don't grudge it him. Perhaps he will pull himself together in some fresh work."

Despite an honest effort to digest *Tannhäuser*, Richard Wagner's music always remained a closed book to Schumann, and his distaste for Wagner's methods gradually developed into an acute prejudice. One of Wagner's avowed aims, for which he spared no trouble, was to induce *musicians* to comprehend his artistic aims and even to share them with him: but with Schumann they made no headway; Wagner's wealth of musical colour meant nothing to him, and the Wagner melodic line was unsympathetic to him. Add to this that Schumann's sense of drama was essentially undramatic, and we have a fairly prickly barrier between the outlooks of the two composers—even without the need of recalling Wagner's criticism of Schumanns' *D minor symphony* as *banal*.

It seems likely that in every progression of Wagner's music, and in every dramatic climax, Schumann realized an abrupt contradiction of his own theories, and contradiction was a thing he could ill brook. In later life he showed this in a somewhat unusual manner ; indeed, if he asked a question, and the answer displeased him, he would turn his back and walk away without further word.

Adverse criticism always provoked him, occasionally beyond the limits of discretion. Here is a letter he wrote to a young man who made him the offer of a libretto, and who, in making it, took the opportunity of tendering a little advice on the subject of romanticism in music : (Sept., 1851) " Although I appreciate your readiness in placing your *Beatrice* libretto before me, I must take exception to your letter, which, in view of our respective positions, is a piece of presumption. You have given no proof of critical acumen, but you send advice such as might be given to a beginner, to a man who has at any rate given some proof of capacity. Did that not occur to you ? Your views were not new to me thirty years ago, and ten years ago I taught them to my pupils, etc., etc."

As a teacher at the Leipzig Conservatoire, Schumann was as entirely out of his element as he was, later, as a conductor. His natural predisposition to be non-communicative was against such work ; but in spite of his retiring manner, he clearly realized his own powers as a composer, and did not hesitate to continue working on his own lines irrespective of criticism. Naturally introspective, self-analysis came easy to him. From a letter to a brother composer (May, 1843) : " Some of my older compositions reflect my former stormy life. The man and the musician within me were always trying to speak at once : indeed, I think that is the case still, only I have learned to control myself more, and my art too."

When one reviews the development of Schumann's art, it is strange to meet the following in a letter written quite near the end of his life, after the re-reading of his musical articles that had appeared in the *Neue Zeitschrift* : " It pleases me to find that in the whole period covered by the articles, and since—more than twenty years—I have scarcely modified my artistic views at all." That, however, is one of the contradictions that surprise one in a man who was among the first to recognize that there can be no advance in art without change. Change or no change, his ideal of the art of music was a high one, and he never allowed himself to swerve from it. Appreciation always moved him to express his gratitude ; thus from a letter to a critic (June, 1849) : " Yes, the faculty of making music that carries in it something of the joy and sorrow of our time, has, I think, been given to me in greater measure than to some others. And your endeavour to show your readers the extent to which my music has its roots in the present day, and also the fact of its having a meaning beyond mere sweet sound, gives me real pleasure and spurs me on to higher efforts."

And one of the facts that I hope to have succeeded in establishing, is that, whether in sickness or in health, this remarkable man did in truth spur himself on with high endeavour until the end. At his best, his music places him among the highest, an adventurer in romance become a rare artist. Capable as he was of devising new forms for new thoughts, he could also throw new thought into old forms, and in that way conjure from the depths of his imagination pearls of great price.

These are the gifts that he left to the world, and they assure him his place in the Temple of Walhalla.

In conclusion let me say that I well realize that nothing that can now be written can add or detract from the artistic value of Robert

Schumann's music on which the critics for upward of a century have sharpened their tusks.

My aim, however, has been to marshal the facts of his life, and to derive from them such conclusions as seemed to me to follow. It has been no part of my plan to draw him larger than life-size ; but rather to try to see him as he was, against a background of the happenings of his time ; and in recounting the events of his life and in sketching the conditions under which he delivered his message, while making no attempt to add a cubit to the stature of the man, it has also been my aim to blot out nothing,

> *nothing extenuate,*
> *Nor set down aught in malice.*

LIST OF ROBERT SCHUMANN'S WORKS

ORCHESTRAL MUSIC

SYMPHONIES

Symphony in B flat. Op. 38
Overture, Scherzo, and Finale. Op. 52
Symphony in C major. Op. 61
Symphony in E♭. Op. 97
Symphony in D minor. Op. 120
Symphony in G (composed 1832-3); not
    published

OVERTURES

Overture to Schiller's *Braut von Messina.* Op. 100
Festival Overture with Chorus on the *Rhein-
    weinlied.* Op. 123
Overture to Shakespeare's *Julius Cæsar.* Op. 128
Overture to Goethe's *Hermann und Dorothea.*
    Op. 136
Overture to the opera *Genoveva.* Op. 81
Overture to Byron's *Manfred.* Op. 115
Overture to *Scenes from Goethe's Faust*

CONCERTOS WITH ORCHESTRA

Concerto for Piano and Orchestra (A minor).
    Op. 54
Concertstück for four Horns and Orchestra.
    Op. 86

SCHUMANN

Introduction and Allegro appassionato.
Concertstück for Piano and Orchestra (G major).
Op. 92
Concerto for Cello and Orchestra. Op. 129
Fantasie for Violin and Orchestra. Op. 131
Concert-allegro, with Introduction; for Piano
and Orchestra (D minor). Op. 134
Concerto for Violin and Orchestra (1853):
unpublished

CHAMBER MUSIC

Three Quartets for two Violins, Viola, and
Cello. Op. 41
Quintet for Piano, two Violins, Viola, and
Cello. Op. 44
Quartet for Piano, Violin, Viola, and Cello.
Op. 47
Trio for Piano, Violin, and Cello (D minor).
Op. 63
Adagio and Allegro for Piano and Horn (ad lib.
Cello and Violin). Op. 70
Fantasiestücke for Piano and Clarinet (ad lib.
Violin or Cello), three pieces. Op. 73
Trio for Piano, Violin, and Cello (F. major).
Op. 80
Fantasiestücke for Piano, Violin, and Cello (four
pieces). Op. 88
Three Romances for Piano and Oboe (ad lib.
Violin or Cello). Op. 94

Stücke im Volkston for Piano and Cello (five)
(ad lib. Violin). Op. 102
Sonata for Piano and Violin (A minor). Op. 105
Trio for Piano, Violin, and Cello (G. minor).
Op. 110
Märchenbilder : four pieces for Piano and Viola
(ad lib. Violin). Op. 113
Sonata for Piano and Violin (D minor). Op. 121
Märchenerzählungen : four pieces for Piano,
Clarinet (ad lib. Violin) and Viola. Op. 132
Experimental String Quartet (1838) : un-
published

CANTATAS, ETC., FOR SOLO VOICES, CHORUS AND
ORCHESTRA

Paradise and the Peri. Op. 50
Adventlied, by Rückert. Op. 71
A Song of Parting. Op. 84
Requiem for Mignon, from Goethe's *Wilhelm
Meister*. Op. 98*b*
Nachtlied, by Hebbel. Op. 108
The Pilgrimage of the Rose. Op. 112
Der Königssohn ; ballad by Uhland. Op. 116
Des Sängers Fluch ; ballad after Uhland. Op. 139
Vom Pagen und der Königstochter: four ballads
by Geibel. Op. 140
Der Glück von Edenhall : ballad by Uhland.
Op. 143
New Year's Song, by Rückert. Op. 144
Mass. Op. 147

Requiem. Op. 148
Scenes from Goethe's *Faust*
An Aria and Chorus for an opera planned upon
Byron's *The Corsair* : unpublished

WORKS FOR THE STAGE: FOR SOLO VOICES,
CHORUS AND ORCHESTRA

Genoveva : opera in four acts. Op. 81
Music to Byron's *Manfred*. Op. 115

SONGS WITH PIANO ACCOMPANIMENTS

Liederkreis, by Heinrich Heine (nine songs).
Op. 24
Myrthen, in four books (twenty-six songs).
Op. 25
Lieder und Gesänge. Op. 27 (five songs)
Three poems by Geibel. Op. 30
Three Poems by Chamisso. Op. 31
Twelve Poems by Justinus Kerner, in two books.
Op. 35
Six Poems by Reinick. Op. 36.
Twelve Poems by Rückert, from *Liebesfrühling*.
Op. 37 (Nos. 2, 4, and 11 were composed by
Clara Schumann)
Liederkreis : twelve poems by Eichendorff.
Op. 39
Five Songs. Op. 40
Frauen-Liebe und Leben : a cycle of songs by
Chamisso. Op. 42

Three Romances and Ballads. Op. 45
Dichterliebe : cycle of songs by Heinrich Heine,
in two books (sixteen songs). Op. 48
Romances and Ballads (three). Op. 53
Belsatzar : ballad by Heinrich Heine. Op. 57
Romances and Ballads (three). Op. 64
Leider und Gesänge (five). Op. 77
Album of Songs for the Young (twenty-nine).
Op. 79
Three Songs. Op. 83
Der Handschuh : ballad by Schiller. Op. 87
Six Songs by Willfried von der Nenn. Op. 89
Six Poems by Lenau, and Requiem (old Catholic
poem). Op. 90
Three Songs from Byron's *Hebrew Melodies*.
Op. 95 ; with accompaniment for Piano-
forte or Harp.
Lieder und Gesänge (five). Op. 96
Lieder und Gesänge from Goethe's *Wilhelm
Meister* (nine). Op. 98a
Seven Songs by Elisabeth Külmann. Op. 104
Six Songs. Op. 107
Four Husarenlieder, by Lenau. Op. 117
Three Poems from the *Wildlieder* of Pfarrius.
Op. 119
Five Happy Songs. Op. 125
Lieder und Gesänge (five). Op. 127
Five Poems by Mary Stuart. Op. 135
Four Songs. Op. 142
Der Deutsche Rhein ; patriotic song by N.
Becker (with chorus)

SONG-CYCLES AND PART-SONGS

Three Poems by Geibel (the first for two Sopranos,
the second for three Sopranos, and the third
(Gipsy Life) for small Chorus, with Triangle
and Tambourines). Op. 29
Four Duets for Soprano and Tenor. Op. 34
Three Two-part Songs. Op. 43
Spanisches Liederspiel : a cycle of nine songs,
with one as an appendix, for several voices.
Op. 74
Four Duets for Soprano and Tenor. Op. 78
Minnespiel, from Rückert's *Liebesfrühling*, for
several voices (eight numbers). Op. 101
Mädchenlieder, by Elisabeth Külmann, for two
Soprano voices. Op. 103
Three Songs for three female voices. Op. 114
Spanische Liebeslieder : a cycle of ten songs for
several voices with four-hand accompaniment
on the Piano. Op. 138

FOR UNACCOMPANIED CHOIR

Six four-part Songs for men's voices. Op. 33
Five Songs by Burns for mixed chorus. Op. 55
Four Songs for mixed chorus. Op. 59
Three Songs for male chorus. Op. 62
Seven Ritornelle, by Rückert, in canon form, for
men's voices. Op. 65
Five Romances und Ballads for chorus. Op. 67
Six Romances for female voices, with Piano
accompaniment ad lib. Op. 69

Five Romances and Ballads for chorus. Op. 75
Six Romances for female voices, with Piano
    accompaniment ad lib. Op. 91
Motet: Verzweifle nicht im Schmerzensthal, by
    Rückert, for double male chorus (Organ
    accompaniment ad lib.). Op. 93
Five Hunting Songs, for male chorus (with an
    ad lib. accompaniment for four Horns).
    Op. 137
Four Songs for double chorus. Op. 141
Five Romances and Ballads for chorus. Op. 145
Five Romances and Ballads for chorus. Op. 146

PIANOFORTE MUSIC

SOLOS

Variations on the name "Abegg." Op. 1
Papillons: twelve short pieces. Op. 2
Studies after Paganini's Caprices. Op. 3
Intermezzi, two books. Op. 4
Impromptus, being variations on a theme by
    Clara Wieck. Op. 5
Davidsbündlertänze. Op. 6: eighteen charac-
    teristic pieces.
Toccata. Op. 7
Allegro. Op. 8
Carnaval. Op. 9: twenty-one pieces
Second set of Studies after Paganini's Caprices.
    Op. 10: six pieces

Sonata in F♯ minor. Op. 11
Fantasiestücke. Op. 12 : two books
Etudes in the form of variations (Etudes symphoniques). Op. 13
Sonata in F minor. Op. 14
Kinderscenen. Op. 15 : thirteen pieces
Kreisleriana. Op. 16 : eight pieces
Fantasia. Op. 17
Arabeske. Op. 18
Blumenstück. Op. 19
Humoreske. Op. 20
Novelletten. Op. 21 : four books
Sonata in G minor. Op. 22
Nachtstücke. Op. 23
Faschingsschwank aus Wien. Op. 26
Three Romances. Op. 28
Scherzo, Gigue, Romanze and Fughette. Op. 32
Album for the Young. Op. 68 : forty pieces
Four Fugues. Op. 72
Four Marches. Op. 76
Waldscenen. Op. 82 : nine pieces
Bunte Blätter. Op. 99 : fourteen pieces
Three Fantasiestücke. Op. 111
Three Sonatas for the Young. Op. 118
Album Leaves. Op. 124 : twenty pieces
Seven pieces in fughetta form. Op. 126
Morning Songs (Gesänge der Frühe). Op. 133 : five pieces.
Scherzo. No. 12 of the posthumous works, originally belonging to the F minor Sonata. Op. 14)

Presto passionato. Op. 22: published as No. 13
of the posthumous works (originally the last
movement of the G minor Sonata)
Piano Accompaniments to Bach's Suites and
Sonatas for Violin
Sonata in B minor (composed 1832): unpub-
lished
Fragment of a Piano Concerto (composed 1832)

DUETS

Bilder aus Osten. Op. 66: six pieces
Twelve Duets for Children large and small.
Op. 85
Ballscenen. Op. 109: nine pieces
Kinderball. Op. 130: six pieces in dance form

DUETS FOR TWO PIANOS

Andante and Variations. Op. 46

PIECES FOR PEDAL PIANO OR ORGAN

Studies for the pedal Piano. Op. 56: six pieces
in canon form
Four Sketches for the pedal Piano. Op. 58
Six Fugues on the name B.A.C.H. Op. 60

INCIDENTAL MUSIC

to *Schön Hedwig*: ballad by Hebbel, for Piano.
Op. 106

to *Ballade vom Haideknabe* : by Hebbel, for
　　Piano.　Op. 122 No. 1
to *The Fugitives* : ballad by Shelley, for Piano.
　　Op. 122, No. 2

JUVENILIA (unpublished)

circa 1825.　A setting of the 150th Psalm for
　　Voices and Instruments
1827.　Songs to his own verses
1828.　Eight Polonaises for Piano, for four hands
1828.　Quartet for Strings and Piano
1828.　Songs to Byron's verses

SOME CONTEMPORARY PRODUCTIONS.	DATE.	SOME SCHUMANN COMPOSITIONS.
Beethoven's *Seventh Symphony*	1814	
Schubert's *Erl König* and other songs	1815	
Carl Löwe's *Erl König, Edward*, etc.	1818	
Spontini's Opera *Olympie*	1821	
Weber's opera *Der Freischütz*	1821	
Spohr's opera *Jessonda*	1822	
Beethoven's *Ninth Symphony*	1823	
The last Beethoven piano sonatas	1823	
Schubert's waltzes for piano	1823	
Schubert's *Die Schöne Müllerin* cycle	1823	
Moscheles' 24 Etudes for piano	1825/6	
The last Beethoven string quartets	1826	
Mendelssohn's *Midsummer Night's Dream* over-ture	1826	
Weber's opera, *Oberon*	1826	
Schubert's *Winterreise* cycle	1827	
Auber's opera *Masaniello*	1828	
Marschner's opera *Der Vampyr*	1828	
Chopin's second piano concerto	1828	
Rossini's opera *William Tell*	1829	Opus 1. piano *variations on A.B.E.G.G.*
Mendelssohn's first *songs without words*	1830	*Papillons* for piano

Hérold's opera, Zampa	1831	*Allegro di bravura for piano*
Bellini's opera *La Sonambula*	1831	
Meyerbeer's opera *Robert le Diable*	1831	
Spohr's Symphony *Die Wiehe der Töne*	1832	
Rossini's *Stabat Mater*	1832	*Six Intermezzi for piano*
Bellini's opera, *Norma*	1832	
	1834	*Carnaval :* scenes for piano
Donizetti's opera *Lucia di Lammermoor*	1835	*Piano sonata F♯ minor*
	1835	*Etudes symphonique*
Mendelssohn's oratorio *St. Paul*	1836	*F minor piano sonata*
Meyerbeer's Opera *Les Huguenots*	1836	*Fantasie for piano*
Mendelssohn's second piano concerto	1837	*Davidsbündlertänze for piano*
Mendelssohn's *Organ Preludes and Fugues*	1837	*Fantasiestücke for piano*
Sterndale Bennett's *C minor piano concerto*	1837	
	1838	*Kinderscenen, Kreisleriana* and *Novelletten*
	1839	*Humoreske* and *Three Romances* for piano
Mendelssohn's *Lobegesang*	1840	Schumann's Year of Song
Donizetti's opera, *Lucrezia Borgia*	1840	
Hiller's oratorio, *Die Zerstörung Jerusalems*	1840	
	1841	*Symphony in B flat, Symphony in D minor, Fantasie for piano and orchestra*
Wagner's opera *Rienzi*	1842	*Three string quartets, Piano quintet, Piano quartet and trio*

259

Some Contemporary Productions.	Date.	Some Schumann Compositions.
Wagner's opera *Der fliegende Holländer*	1843	*Andante and variations* for two pianos
Donizetti's opera *Don Pasquale*	1843	*Paradise and the Peri*
Robert Franz's first book of songs	1843	Transfiguration scene from *Faust*
Berlioz's *Carnaval Romain*	1844	
Verdi's opera, *Ernani*	1844	The piano concerto
Spohr's last opera *Die Kreuzfahrer*	1845	Fugal and contrapuntal music
Wagner's opera *Tannhäuser*	1845	
Cézar Franck's oratorio *Ruth*	1846	*C major Symphony*
	1847	Two piano trios
	1848	*Manfred*
	1849	The opera *Genoveva*; Spanisches Liederspiel : Spanische Liebes-Lieder
Wagner's opera *Lohengrin*	1850	Scenes from Faust completed : overture, Bride of Messina : The Rhenish Symphony
Verdi's opera, *Rigoletto*	1851	The Pilgrimage of the Rose : Choral ballads
Gounod's first opera, *Sapho*	1851	Rheinweinlied
	1852	The Mass : The Requiem : Nachtlied
Brahm's C major piano sonata, and Quartet Op. 1	1853	Overture to the *Scenes from Faust*

INDEX

261

INDEX

INDEX

INDEX

INDEX

INDEX

INDEX

INDEX